WreckProtect

Decay and protection of archaeological wooden shipwrecks

Partners

SP Technical Research Institute of Sweden
Charlotte Gjelstrup Björdal, Coordinator

National Museum of Denmark, Denmark
David Gregory

Cultural Heritage Agency, the Netherlands
Martijn Manders

The Geological Survey of Denmark and Greenland, Denmark
Zyad Al Hamdani

GEUS

University of Gothenburg, Sweden
Jon Havenhand, Christin Appelqvist

The Viking Ship Museum, Roskilde, Denmark
Jørgen Dencker

External Advisory Group
Stefan Wessman, National Board of Antiquities, Finland
Friedrich Lüth, German Archaeological Institute, Germany
Giulia Boetto, Centre Camille Julian, France

European Commission
Directorate General Research
Directorate I - Environment
Michel Chapuis (project officer)

WreckProtect

Decay and protection of archaeological wooden shipwrecks

*Edited by Charlotte Gjelstrup Björdal & David Gregory
with assistance from Athena Trakadas*

SEVENTH FRAMEWORK
PROGRAMME

WreckProtect
Decay and protection of archaeological wooden shipwrecks
edited by Charlotte Gjelstrup Björdal & David Gregory
with assistance from Athena Trakadas

Published by Archaeopress Ltd
Gordon House
276 Banbury Road
Oxford OX2 7ED
www.archaeopress.com

Book and cover design, DTP, copy editing, and language consultant:
Athena Trakadas, Viking Ship Museum, Roskilde, Denmark

Printed on acid-free paper

FSC
www.fsc.org
MIX
Paper from
responsible sources
FSC® C013262

ISBN 978-1-905739-48-6

Published with support from:
European Commission, Directorate Environment, FP 7

Printed in England by Information Press, Oxford

Front cover images: A diver with the 17th-century Stinesminde wreck, Mariager Fjord, Denmark (photo: S.E. Jørgensen; © Viking Ship Museum); Shipworm damage to a piece of wood (photo: David Gregory)

Back cover images: Map of monthly frequency of shipworm occurrence in the Baltic predicted for 2009-2020 (image: Christin Appelqvist); Decay of wood cell walls by erosion bacteria, SEM-photo (photo: Charlotte Gjelstrup Björdal); David Gregory setting protective debris netting over a shipwreck site (photo: Jørgen Dencker)

Contents

Preface

Charlotte Gjelstrup Björdal & David Gregory

Over the past few decades the international community of marine archae-ologists and conservators has moved toward the *in-situ* preservation of wooden shipwrecks, as opposed to excavation and conservation. Amongst other things, this interest reflects the awareness and understanding that underwater degradation processes endanger the long-term stability of shipwrecks, and that a wreck found today may be lost tomorrow, or in the near future. Excavating each unique wreck is not a realistic option mainly because of the tremendous costs for excavation, conservation, storage, and exhibition. In order to assure that future generations will also have the opportunity to explore and investigate shipwrecks from the past, we have an obligation and possibility to secure some of these unique traces from the past by long-term protection *in situ*. This is recommended as a first choice option by the *2001 UNESCO Convention on the Protection of the Submerged Cultural Heritage*.

Literature and up-to-date knowledge on wood decay processes in ma-rine and other aquatic environments have not been readily obtainable for managers, archaeologists, conservators and other stakeholders working in the field of cultural heritage. It is, however, obvious that this knowledge is essential if we should be able to protect wrecks in an efficient and sus-tainable way. "You have to know your enemy, in order to beat them" – in practice, the way of "defeating them" is to use, develop and refine meth-ods for *in-situ* protection. Today there are protection methods that have been randomly tested and used, but very few long-term evaluations have taken place and few standards have been established.

The **WreckProtect** project started in 2009 and was funded by the Euro-pean Commission's *Seventh Framework Programme* (Environment) (FP7-ENV-2008-1 No. 226225). It was an inter- and cross-disciplinary coordina-tion action involving partners with expertise in Geographical Information Systems (GIS), marine biology, wood microbiology, marine archaeology and conservation. The project was dedicated to investigating the long-term preservation of the unique well-preserved shipwrecks situated in the brackish waters of the Baltic Sea. It focussed on studying the decay caused by and spread of the marine borer *Teredo navalis*, as well as on as-sessing methods suitable for *in-situ* protection. In the first chapter of the book, the project is further introduced.

The obtained knowledge and outcome from this project have provid-ed the basis of this book, which contains chapters on different scientific aspects related to degradation and protection of submerged shipwrecks.

Some additional chapters, such as those on the structure of wood, have been added in order to make a more complete and useful handbook. The book is not a complete story of all processes taking place on and affecting shipwrecks in marine and brackish waters. It does, however, include the most important biological and physical factors that endanger the long-term preservation of wooden shipwrecks.

We hope that this book will be useful for stakeholders of underwater cultural heritage, marine archaeologists, conservators, engineers, and not least, students in related fields at universities around and outside Europe. Despite the fact that this book focuses on shipwrecks in the Baltic Sea, the decay processes there are similar to other marine waters around the world. The main difference is principally the presence of a much larger spectrum and diversity of aggressive marine borers and crustaceans in subtropical and tropical waters. Therefore the methods for physical protection are adaptable to most waters worldwide.

This monograph is a co-production of the consortium of **WreckProtect**, coordinated and edited by the management team. In addition, the external advisory group and specialists from outside the project have contributed to certain chapters of this book.

Without the financial support from the European Commission, this work would not have been possible. We would therefore like to express our gratitude to the European Commission, Environment Directorate, who in the context of the Seventh Framework Programme funded the **Wreck-Protect** project with the aim of reinforcing the scientific and technical basis for protecting and conserving European patrimony.

SEVENTH FRAMEWORK
PROGRAMME

1. Introduction

Charlotte Gjelstrup Björdal & David Gregory

1.1 Introduction to the project

Throughout history, a large number of wooden ships have been built, used, abandoned on the foreshores of coasts, and wrecked at sea. Communication and trade took place over large distances, meaning that a ship built in one of the Scandinavian countries could end up far away from its home destination. Today the remains of these ships, shipwrecks from different historical periods, can be found in marine and freshwater environments world-wide. Their origins are always a matter of great interest and research potential for marine archaeologists.

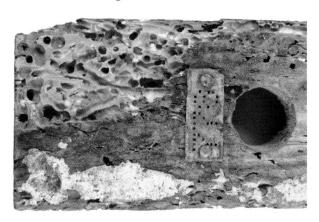

Fig. 1.1. Heavy attack by Teredo navalis. *The mollusc penetrates and digests the wood, forming up to 1 cm-wide tunnels (photo: C. Gjelstrup Björdal).*

Most of the wooden ships that were sailed and used in the past, since their sinking, have undergone deterioration by natural decay processes. Wood is turned into carbon, oxygen, and hydrogen as a part of the carbon cycle. These processes are mainly of a biological nature, where specialised micro-organisms together with aggressive marine boring molluscs and crustaceans in waters world-wide are able to turn the once strong timbers of a shipwreck into very fragile material that only resembles the original wood in appearance. This deterioration, in the right conditions, can happen within a short period of time – taking decades rather than centuries. Shipworms, *Teredo sp.*, are one of the most aggressive bivalves (mussels) that settle on wooden surfaces as small free-swimming larvae. The larvae develop and bore into the wood, where the adult animal, which can be 60-100 cm in length, spends its entire life within the wooden structure. It then bores perfectly round tunnels throughout the inside of the wood, which it digests (**Fig. 1.1**). Due to a combination of this biological degradation, and the physical action of currents and underwater sediment erosion, the wood can be further fragmented and spread into the environment, ultimately to be broken down by micro-organisms. These processes take place in most of the oceans and seas world-wide, including the Mediterranean, the North Sea and the Atlantic Ocean that surrounds Europe. Bearing this in mind, intact historical shipwrecks are therefore a rare occurrence.

One place where such degradation is fortunately not the case is the Baltic Sea. The Baltic Sea is a brackish marine environment and one of the few seas in the world containing a unique and well-preserved collection of shipwrecks, submerged archaeological sites of earlier settlements, and other coastal maritime constructions. In total, nine countries share this exclusive archive of historical and archaeological information from the past. Today it is estimated that there are up to 100,000 shipwrecks in the Baltic, of which at least 6,000 are deemed of significant archaeological and historical significance. New wrecks are discovered each year and consequently the number of known wrecks is still rising. The brackish water has excluded the aggressive marine borers, and this is the reason why historical shipwrecks can be found more or less complete both above and beneath the seabed. The raised shipwreck *Vasa*, the number one tourist attraction of Stockholm, Sweden, is an example of the unique preservation conditions in the Baltic Sea region (**Fig. 1.2**).

Excavating and raising all of these wrecks is not a realistic option in the first instance due to the tremendous costs for excavation, conservation, storage, and display. Consequently, *in-situ* preservation has become an alternative to excavation as way of long-term preservation and is also recommended as a first choice option by the *2001 UNESCO Convention on the Protection of the Submerged Cultural Heritage*.

A previous European Community Culture 2000 Programme, *Monitoring, Safeguarding and Visualizing North-European Shipwreck Sites* (MoSS), notes that new attacks by marine borers were found at shipwreck sites along the north coast of Germany at Rügen, an area that had not previously been affected by shipworm (Jöns 2003). This information, together with other observations on attacks in wooden harbour pilings along the east coast of Denmark as well as the southwest coast of Sweden, raised the questions: was the shipworm *Teredo navalis* spreading into new areas of the Baltic Sea, and could a massive loss of unique archaeological shipwrecks and submerged settlements with wooden finds then be expected? Furthermore, could there be a possible relationship between the shipworm spread and global climate change?

Based on this, a two-year project, **WreckProtect**, funded by the European Commission, started in 2009. The full title of the project is: "***Strategies for the protection of shipwrecks in the Baltic Sea against forthcoming attack by wood degrading marine borers. A synthesis and information project based on the effects of climatic changes***". It was financed

Fig. 1.2. The warship
Vasa displayed at
the Vasa Museum in
Stockholm, Sweden
(photo courtesy Vasa
Museum).

mainly by the European Commission within the Seventh Framework Programme and coordinated by SP Technical Research Institute of Sweden.
The cross-disciplinary scientific project involved geophysicists, marine bi-
ologists, marine archaeologists, wood scientists, and conservators from
three countries: the Netherlands, Denmark, and Sweden. The external advisory board consisted of three marine archaeologists representing Germany, Finland, and France.

1.2 Objectives and main achievements

The objective of **WreckProtect** was to secure the preservation of two important objects of cultural heritage in marine environments against attack
by shipworms: namely shipwrecks and submerged archaeological settlements. Two questions were in focus:

    1) How can we predict the spread of shipworm in the Baltic Sea so
that cultural heritage can be preserved before any eventual invasion?

    2) Which physical methods are available and could be used for protect-
ing these sites where they lie, *in situ*?

As there was a lack of scientific information on the spread of ship-worm, the first objective was to find a way to predict the actual spread today. For this purpose, environmental data from the Baltic Sea were used to develop a GIS model that could indicate areas in the sea where possible attacks could be expected. The GIS maps were based on crucial environmental parameters for the survival and reproduction of shipworms. The most important parameters identified were temperature, salinity, oxygen concentrations and water currents. When the GIS model was available, data connected with future climate change models were added, and the prediction of future spreads were attempted.

Various methods for protecting shipwrecks and historical settlements *in situ* have been tested and used during the last 20-30 years. These methods were mainly aimed at protection against shipworm attack and sediment erosion. With the help of literature studies and a seminar, methods used in the past and present were critically evaluated.

Two guidelines, aimed at archaeologists, conservators and resource managers were synthesised as a result of this research:

1) A guideline providing cultural resource managers, archaeologists, and conservators responsible for the long-term preservation of cultural heritage with tools for assessing and predicting the future spread of *Teredo navalis* in the Baltic Sea.

2) A guideline for recommendation of practical methods for protection of wrecks and historical settlements *in situ*.

The use of guidelines for the prediction of risk areas in the Baltic Sea that are in imminent threat of attack by *Teredo navalis* will, for the first time, make it possible to forecast an attack. The methods available for efficient *in-situ* preservation have been evaluated, and these actions are related to principal cost-benefit analyses. The guidelines are meant to be user-friendly and serve as tools for stakeholders and end-users to ensure the protection of unique submerged cultural heritage sites for future generations.

Although a pressing problem in the Baltic, wood-boring organisms are also ubiquitous in northwest Europe, the Mediterranean and other major oceans and are therefore a threat to marine archaeological sites throughout the world. Thus it should be stressed that even though the **Wreck-Protect** project has focused upon the situation in the Baltic Sea, the results and guidelines are relevant to the protection of wooden shipwrecks and submerged archaeological settlements wherever there is a threat of shipworms.

2. The Baltic Sea: a unique resource of underwater cultural heritage

2.1 An archive under water
David Gregory & Martijn Manders

The Baltic Sea is relatively young from a geological perspective; it was formed approximately 15,000 years ago and has existed in its present form for the past 3,000 years. Since prehistoric times climatic changes have affected the maritime environment of the Baltic Sea, influencing and shaping the lives of the people living on its shores. In historic and more recent times, it has been a major region of seafaring, intricately linking the populations of the nine countries that border it during times of maritime trade and warfare. For millennia, the Baltic Sea has provided the region with the means of communication, transport and food.

It is therefore not surprising that the Baltic Sea is a rich source of underwater cultural heritage from prehistoric times to the present. The bottom of the Baltic Sea is effectively a submerged cultural landscape, with remnants of millennia of human activity including Stone-Age settlements and fish traps from the people living around the shores of the sea. Furthermore, because of melting ice, the once terrestrial landscape was inundated with water, submerging large amounts of forest, which can still be found in the southern and southwestern parts of the Baltic Sea.

In the open Baltic Sea the remains of wooden shipwrecks, many of them hundreds of years old, often sit upright with masts and rigging still intact. Closer to shore lie the remains of wooden harbour installations and other constructions designed to prevent the passage of ships.

In this respect, the Baltic Sea is a giant underwater museum, with many well preserved remains surviving because of the brackish water limiting the predation of shipworms. These remains often are linked not just to one country, or exclusively the countries around the Baltic Sea, but to the whole of Europe and even beyond.

This museum is bordered and curated by nine different nations: Denmark, Sweden, Finland, the Russian Federation, Estonia, Latvia, Lithuania, Poland, and Germany. The *Rutilus Project*, a joint project involving all the above-listed countries, sought to develop strategies for the sustainable development of the underwater cultural heritage in the Baltic Sea region (Anon. 2006). As part of this project, the Sites and Monuments Registers of the various countries were used to show the wealth of known underwater cultural heritage in the Baltic. As of 2006 there were approximately

20,000 known underwater cultural sites in the Baltic region; about 9,000 of these were designated monuments and protected under national or federal cultural heritage laws (normally, protected monuments have to be over 100 years old). **Table 2.1** shows the breakdown of the number of underwater sites in the various territorial waters of the countries bordering the Baltic Sea and **Fig. 2.1** shows the distribution of these sites.

Table 2.1. Number of wrecks in the Baltic Sea region (from the Rutilus Project, Anon. 2006).

Country	Number of underwater sites in the Baltic Sea
Denmark	3,781 protected (Baltic Sea) and 7,247 known sites (North Sea/Baltic Sea)
Estonia	13 protected and 200 registered sites
Finland	728 protected and 1,074 registered sites
Finland: Åland	148 protected and 500 registered sites
Germany: Mecklenburg – Western Pomerania	1,000 known sites (lakes and sea)
Germany: Schleswig – Holstein	0 protected and 150 registered sites
Latvia	0 protected and 323 registered sites
Lithuania	5 protected and 20 registered sites
Poland	1 protected and 65 registered sites
Russian Federation	20 protected and 200 registered sites
Sweden	3,218 protected and 8,300 registered sites; 3,482 known historical wreck losses

References

Anonymous, 2006. *Rutilus: Strategies for a Sustainable Development of the Underwater Cultural Heritage in the Baltic Sea Region.* Report dbr 1267/03-51 (Stockholm, Swedish Maritime Museums).
Anonymous, 2003. *Treasures of the Baltic Sea. A hidden wealth of culture.* Report number 46 (Stockholm, Swedish Maritime Museums).
Lindström, M. (ed.), 1998. *The Marine Archaeology of the Baltic Sea Area. Conditions in the present, possibilities and problems in the future. Proceedings of the first meeting of the International Marine Archaeological Conference of the Baltic Sea* (Stockholm, Södertörns Högskola Research Reports 1).

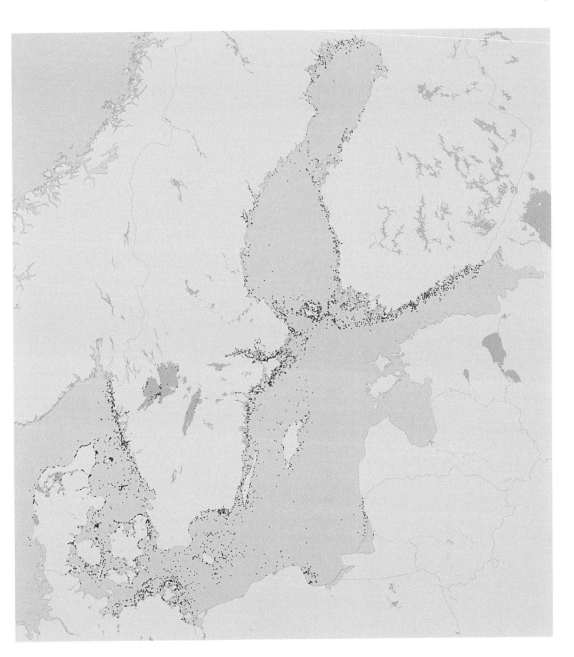

Fig. 2.1. Distribution of registered underwater cultural heritage sites located in Danish, German, Swedish, Finnish, Polish and Lithuanian waters and waters surrounding the Åland Islands of Finland. Site locations in Estonia, the Russian Federation and Latvia are approximate (courtesy/©: Landesamt für Kultur und Denkmalpflege, Abteilung Archäologie und Denkmalpflege, Schwerin).

2.2 Case studies
David Gregory

Generally, wrecks are currently best preserved in the inner-most parts of the Baltic where the water has been too brackish to support shipworm. In the more westerly parts of the Baltic shipworm has attacked those parts of wrecks which are exposed and generally they are more poorly preserved. This section gives a few examples of the variation of preservation that can be found in the Baltic.

2.2.1 *Vrouw Maria*
Stefan Wessman

Vrouw Maria was a Dutch-owned merchant vessel mainly used for carrying cargo from Amsterdam to St. Petersburg, but it also made at least one journey to Lisbon. The ship would have probably fallen into oblivion among thousands of its kind if it hadn't been for its last journey, which ended in the Finnish Archipelago Sea. Here the ship went down after several days of struggle after damage received during a storm that blew it off-course. On this last journey the ship was carrying boxes containing Dutch works of art bought by Catherine the Great at auction in Amsterdam. The loss of these paintings caused a diplomatic correspondence that attracted the Finnish researcher C. Ahlström's attention some two hundred years later (Ahlström 1979). From that day on, finding the wreck of *Vrouw Maria* became one of the most thrilling goals in Finnish sport-divers' minds. What no one could imagine in the 1970s was the enormous technical development that was going to take place in the next twenty years. By the mid-1990s numerous types of equipment for scanning and mapping the seafloor were available. The possibilities to look for a wreck in a defined area were available and the first real attempt to find *Vrouw Maria* was successful in 1999.

The wreck is located in the southern part of the Archipelago Sea and rests at a maximum depth of 41 m. The wreck and scattered parts from it cover approximately a 1,500 m² area. The wreck stands on its keel with the hull intact except for some missing planks above the hatch in the aft of the ship (**Fig. 2.2**). The rudder was lost in the storm when the ship ran aground, taking a part of the transom with it; the rest of the transom has disintegrated and lies on the seafloor behind the ship. The coach roof is also missing; this is probably a result of the sinking/wrecking process, the same phenomenon can be seen on several other wrecks. The main part of the deck planks is *in situ* but there are gaps and holes in many places. Aft of the main-mast is a crushed deckhouse lying in a pile on deck. The main- and fore-masts are still standing while the top-masts together with the

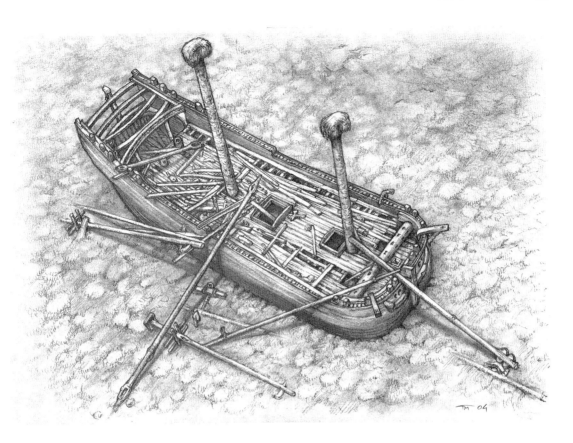

Fig. 2.2. Perspective drawing of Vrouw Maria *(Tiina Miettinen, National Board of Antiquities, Finland).*

yards have fallen down onto the deck and the seafloor on the starboard side of the wreck. The bow sprit is tilted toward the seafloor with the jib boom lying adjacent. The hatches are open and the hold is filled with cargo almost to the deck level. The length of the wreck is 26.34 m from the outer edge of the stem to the outer edge of the stern at the height of the coach roof beams and the maximum beam is 7.10 m over the railings amidships. The deck is about 4 m above the seafloor while the stem and stern rise 5 m and 6 m above the floor, respectively. The main-mast rises approximately 19 m and the fore-mast 17 m above the seafloor. There is very little sedimentation at the site but some of the construction details behind and on the starboard side of the wreck are partially buried in sediment (Wessman 2003; Wessman 2004).

From the summer of 2001 *Vrouw Maria* was part of a three-year EU project, *Monitoring, Safeguarding and Visualizing North-European Shipwreck Sites (MoSS): Common European Underwater Cultural Heritage – Challenges for Cultural Resource Management*. Within the project, biological wood-degrading factors were studied by installing wooden samples at the site. As expected there was no wood-borer activity present at the site; instead, the main threats are soft rot and bacteria that infected the samples already after 3 months (Leino et al. 2011; Palma 2004).

The hull in a ship like this is typically of oak and the rigging of conifers; this has been confirmed by analyses of wood samples from the hull. Samples of the rigging are pine. Deck planks have not yet been analysed, nor have other elements of the ship. The bulkheads under deck are heavily eroded – there are only fragments of them left. Wood of low quality was often used for bulkheads in ships at this time and the poor state of preservation indicates that this was also the case in *Vrouw Maria*.

In an almost completely preserved ship there are wooden fragments and ship timbers in all sizes – from tiny parrel beads to substantial timbers like the stems and the masts. The smallest wooden pieces are only a few centimetres, while the main-mast, for example, is 18-19 m long and has a circumference of 1.48 m just above deck level. Different types of planks come in all sizes, with their thicknesses varying from under a centimetre in the wooden crates to 5 cm in the hull planking.

The wreck of *Vrouw Maria* has only been known for a little over ten years, which is a very short period when studying decay on a wreck from the time of discovery. It is, however, obvious that the decay on *Vrouw Maria* has accelerated since the wreck was found even if contact with it has been restricted to research diving from the moment that it was found. Damage caused during work on the wreck is as follows: the upper part of the stern was damaged by a surface buoy rope, and the windlass brake pawl was torn off in the same way. The braces of one of the pumps have been knocked off, one of the posts of the deckhouse has been knocked down and a tack block on the outside of the hull fell down to the seafloor – all probably caused by divers' fins. In addition, some wooden parts on the deck have moved from their original position, also probably caused by careless divers.

There is no question that the wreck of *Vrouw Maria* is important from an archaeological point of view. Even if there are several known wrecks of merchantmen from the 18th century, *Vrouw Maria* might be the only known one that has been untouched after discovery. No looting has taken place. In addition to the fascinating story of Catherine the Great's paintings, *Vrouw Maria* represents the normal daily trade that took place between Amsterdam and Russia. Excavation, raising and conservation of the wreck have been periodically discussed since it was found but for the moment there are no plans to do this.

___

References

Ahlström, C., 1979. *Sjunkna Skepp* (Lund, Natur och kultur).
Leino, M., Ruuskanen, A., Flinkman, J., Kaasinen, J., Klemelä, U., Hietala, R., & Nappu, N., 2011. The natural environment of the shipwreck *Vrouw Maria* (1771) in the Northern Baltic Sea: an assessment of her state of preservation. *International Journal of Nautical Archaeology* 40.1: 133-150.

Palma, P., 2004. Final report for the monitoring theme of the MoSS project. In: C.O. Ceder-lund (ed.), *MoSS Final Report* (Helsinki, National Board of Antiquities): 8-37.
Wessman, S. 2003. The documentation and reconstruction of the wreck of *Vrouw Maria*. *MoSS Newsletter* 2003.1: 14-17.
Wessman, S. 2004. The reconstruction of *Vrouw Maria*: Building a ship from upwards down. In: C.O. Cederlund (ed.), *MoSS Final Report* (Helsinki, National Board of Antiquities): 61-63.

2.2.2 "Kraveln". The wreck of an early carvel-built ship at Franska Stenarna, Stockholm Archipelago, Sweden
Jon Adams & Johan Rönnby

In December 1990, the discovery of a wreck below Franska Stenarna ('French Stones'), in the Nämdöfjärd area of the Stockholm Archipelago, caused great excitement in the press. The wreck was quickly identified as *Lybska Svan* ('Swan of Lübeck'), the carvel-built flagship of the fleet as-sembled by Gustav Eriksson Vasa in 1522 to fight the Danes. As "founding father", Gustav Vasa still enjoys iconic status in Sweden.

Maritime archaeological investigations conducted at the site since 1995 have shown that the wreck is not *Lybska Svan* but is in fact a carvel-built warship from the early 16th century. Written sources indicate that in 1525, one of the smaller ships in the king's fleet, after a bloody campaign in Kalmar, wrecked "between Dalarö and Djurshamn in 25 fathoms of wa-ter". The ship is recorded just as one of the king's "*beste kraffweller*" ('one of his best carvels') (Daggfeldt 1963).

Unlike so many Baltic wrecks, the remains of the 'Kravel' no longer con-stitute one integral unit. A considerable amount of the structure survives but much of it is disarticulated. Where total excavation and recovery is not to be carried out, shipwrecks in this condition can reveal information on design and construction of a more detailed nature than hulls that are in-tact simply because they are accessible. Normally wrecks are partially bur-ied in sediment while exposed surface details are obscured or eroded by marine growth. The depth of this wreck prevents the latter, although the timber surfaces have been severely abraded. Tool marks and carpenters marks do not therefore survive on exposed surfaces, although aspects of timber conversion and construction are readily apparent. Notably, vari-ous fittings and many of the principal rigging elements such as masts and spars survive – something that is relatively unusual.

The majority of the hull remains of the now so-called "Kravel/ Kraveln" wreck and its contents came to rest on steeply sloping rock and clay below Franska Stenarna, between c. 30 m and 55 m depth (**Fig. 2.3**). The ship lies on its port side and hangs precariously on a sloping ledge with much of the structure overhanging an even steeper drop to the seabed another 20 m below. Over the centuries the wood has distorted considerably and

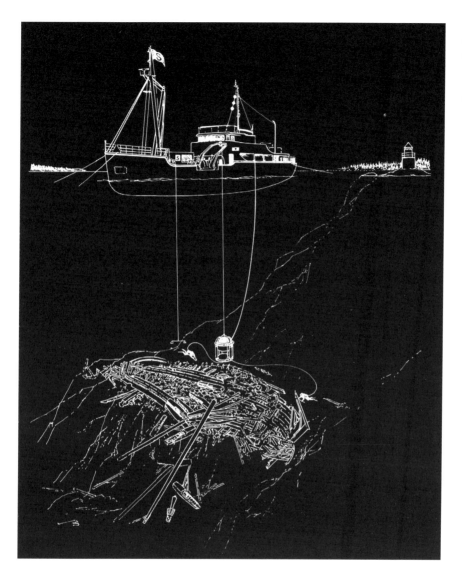

Fig. 2.3. The wreck site at Franska Stenarna with survey vessels above "Kraveln" (drawing: J. Adams).

much of the hull is draped over the contours of the rock (**Fig. 2.4**). This, together with the depth, low light, low temperature and the dislocation of much of the structure make recording a challenging process.

To do so, an array of datum points was installed around the structure and their three-dimensional co-ordinates were established using Nick Rule's Direct Survey Method (DSM) programme (Rule 1989). The coordinates were then used as a control for the production of conventional plans, utilising video and still photography.

Samples of both oak and pine were taken for dendrochronological analysis, but only one sample, from an oak hull plank, was successfully dated. It included sapwood, with the outer-most growth ring dating to 1512. The dendro-curve most closely matched a northern Polish refer-

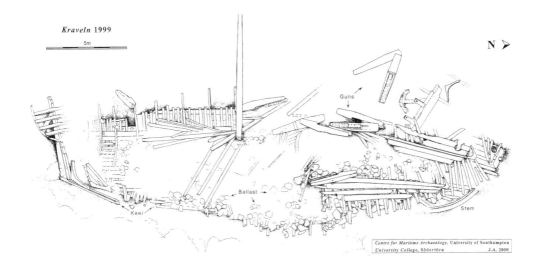

Fig. 2.4. Site plan of "Kraveln" (drawing: J. Adams).

Fig. 2.5. Armament and other artefacts are strewn about the wreck. This is a three-legged cooking pot of copper-alloy (photo: J. Rönnby).

ence chronology and, given the sapwood allowance for trees growing in this region, this result is likely to have been very near the felling date (A. Bråthen, pers. comm.).

Sub-samples of the planks recovered for dendrochronology were sent to Prof. T. Nilsson of the Swedish Agricultural University at Uppsala for microbiological analysis. The aim was to identify strains of fungus whose presence would indicate whether the vessel's timbers were relatively new or had been subject to a degree of degradation. Analysis showed that there were indeed strains of fungus that can only have infested the timber prior to sinking, suggesting the ship was unlikely to have been very new when lost.

Items recovered include several shot of iron and stone, but also artefacts associated with the galley: principally a large cast copper-alloy cauldron and a large copper-alloy cauldron or kettle made from beaten and riveted plates. Both lay below the fallen mast and this may not have been far from their original position, as it is consistent with the location of the galley in other ships of this period. Also recovered were two small three-legged cooking pots, one of copper-alloy and the other of earthenware (**Fig. 2.5**). Undoubtedly, however, the most significant assemblage on the wreck is the collection of wrought iron guns. So far, the number of guns found still attached to their massive wooden carriages is at least 14, while the various sledges, barrels and chambers indicate the total was likely somewhat higher.

In its construction, the vessel in the Nämdöfjärd area exhibits one of the major technological changes observable in the maritime archaeological record of this period: the adoption of the carvel method of ship construction. With regard to size, the keel was between 17-19 m long and the Kraveln's main breadth accordingly would have been around 6.5-7 m with a depth in hold of about 3-3.5 m, consistent with the size of the observed beams. According to English formulae in use some half a century later, capacity would have been around 120-150 tuns (Salisbury 1966). However, tonnage formulae and keel-to-breadth ratios only give a crude indication of size at this time.

As an example of the carvel ships being built in Northern Europe at the time, this vessel is a very valuable addition to the database in terms of ship technology and the general developments in shipping and maritime enterprise of the period. The evidence implicates these ships in the activities of the 'new men' of the age, and this particular one in the state-building enterprise of Gustav Vasa. In this way an investigation of the ship and the associated primary historical documents provide a new means of understanding of the social context in which these technological changes took place.

References

Adams, J., 2003. *Ships, Innovation and Social Change* (Stockholm, University of Stockholm).
Adams, J., Norman, P., & Rönnby, J., 1991. Rapport från marinarkeologisk vrakbesiktning, Franska Stenarna, Nämdöfjärden. *Marinarkeologisk tidskrift* (Stockholm) 2: 8-10.
Adams, J., & Rönnby, J., 1996. *Furstens Fartyg* (Uppsala, Swedish National Maritime Museum).
Adams, J., & Rönnby, J., 1998. *Nämdöfjärdens Kraveln* (Unpublished report, Stockholm County Authority).
Adams, J., & Rönnby, J., 2005. *Nämdöfjärdens Kraveln 2003-4* (Unpublished report, Stockholm County Authority).
Adams, J., & Rönnby, J., 2009. Kraveln – marinarkeologiska undersökningar av ett skeppsvrak från tidig 1500-tal i Nämdöfjärden, Stockholms skärgård. In: K. Schoerner (ed.), *Skärgård och örlog. Nedslag i Stockholms skärgårds tidiga historia* (Stockholm, Kungl. Vitterhets historie och antikvitets akademien): 73-102.
Adams, J. & Rönnby, J., in press. One of his Majesty's 'beste kraffwells'. The wreck of an early carvel-built ship at Franska Stenarna, Sweden. *International Journal of Nautical Archaeology*.

Daggfeldt, B., 1963. Lybska Svan. *Tidskrift I Sjöväsendet*: 3-27.

Glete, J., 1977. Svenska örlogsfartyg 1521-1560. Flottans uppbyggnad under ett tekniskt brytningsskede. *Forum Navale* 31: 23-119.

Glete, J., 1994. *Navies and Nations* (Stockholm, Almqvist & Wiksell International).

Glete, J., 2000. *Warfare at Sea 1500-1650. Maritime Conflicts and the Transformation of Europe* (London, Routledge).

Rule, N., 1989. Direct Survey Method and its Application Underwater. *International Journal of Nautical Archaeology* 18.2: 157-162.

Rönnby, J., & Adams, J., 1994. *Östersjöns Sjunkna Skepp* (Stockholm, Tiden).

Salisbury, W., 1966. Early Tonnage Measurement in England. *Mariner's Mirror* 52.1: 41-51.

2.2.3 The Ghost Ship: a 17th-century Dutch ship on the bottom of the Baltic Sea

Martijn Manders

In 2003 the Swedish dive company, Deep Sea Productions, discovered an extremely well preserved shipwreck in 130 m of water, just north of the island of Gotland. The ship stands proudly upright on its keel. It has now been extensively investigated with remote-sensing equipment such as remotely-operated vehicles (ROVs).

The ship — colloquially called the "Ghost Ship"— has three masts, two of which are still standing. It is a so- called *flute*, probably of Dutch origin and dated to the mid-17th century. This type of ship, and in such condition, has never been encountered before. The ship's timbers and the visible inventory lying on deck all seem to be in very good condition. Only the outer few millimetres of wood have become soft due to microbial decay (**Figs. 2.6 & 2.7**). However, rope and sails have not been found. Probably these parts of the rigging — almost pure cellulose — have completely de-

Fig. 2.6. The Ghost Ship seen towards the helm port. This picture clearly shows the remarkable preservation conditions (photo courtesy Ghost Ship Project).

teriorated over time. The visible iron parts, such as bolts and dead eye chains seem to be corroded as well. Its good state of preservation is mainly because the ship was almost totally constructed of wood and the fact that shipworm (*Teredo navalis*) is absent in the area.

The ship itself is hardly covered by any sedimentation. Only in the hold do we see a fine layer of silt. On the seabed there is also hardly any fine sediment, with the ship standing upright on a hard rocky substrate.

The ship is interesting from a scientific perspective: it can tell us a lot about 17th-century shipbuilding techniques, ship ornament (art), and the socio-economic history of the Baltic, regarding, for example, Dutch trade. Above all, it is a material witness – one can say an icon – for the period of great trade expansion of the Dutch Republic and the important role the Baltic area played in this. It is therefore a typical example of mutual heritage between the Netherlands and Swe-

Fig. 2.7. One pine plank has been raised from the seabed to date it using dendrochronology. The rings suggest a date just after 1631 with a provenance of Gotland (photo courtesy Ghost Ship Project).

den, but maybe even other countries. This may become clearer if more research is carried out.

The Ghost Ship is about 25 m long and 6 m wide. The aft is round and the distance between the sides decreases higher up in the ship. Viewed from the stern, the ship has a pear-like form, which is characteristic for the *flute* type. The cut-out flower motives around the helm port are typical for a 17th-century Dutch ship as are the wooden carvings that look like merchantmen, which were placed high up at each side of the taffrail (the quarter-pieces). One of these carvings has been recovered.

The ship looks typically Dutch. This is not so strange, since the *flute* was probably the most successful Dutch ship designs of its time. Dutch *flutes* were also bought by ship owners from England, France and even the Baltic states. Furthermore, besides the ships, the shipbuilders themselves and their knowledge were a successful export. In the 17[th]century, hundreds of Dutch shipbuilders were working in the Baltic, using their techniques to build the ships they had learned to do in the Dutch style.

References

Deep Sea Productions: http://www.deepsea.se/ (Accessed October, 2011).

Hagberg, B., Dahm, J., & Douglas, C., 2008. *Shipwrecks of the Baltic* (Stockholm, Deep Sea Productions & Prisma).

MACHU Project Wreck ID: http://www.machuproject.eu/machu_cms/index.php?mode =standalone_viewer&wreck_id=64&puid=0 (Accessed October, 2011).

Sleeswyk, A.W., 2003. *De Goudeneeuw van het Fluitschip* (Franeker, Uitgeverij Van Wijnen).

Witsen, N., 1690 (2[nd]edn). *Architecturanavalisetreginemnauticum (Aeloude en hedendaeg- schescheepsbouw en bestier, 1671)* (Amsterdam, Pieter en Joan Blaeu).

2.2.4 *Kronan*

Lars Einarsson

The Swedish Royal ship *Kronan* ('The Royal Crown') exploded and sank off the east coast of Öland in a battle with an allied Danish-Dutch fleet on 1 June, 1676. According to contemporary records, she was one of the largest sailing vessels in Europe. Her dimensions were 178 1/2 ft at the waterline, 197 ft overall with a 43 1/2 ft beam, with a calculated displacement of 2,300 cubic metric tons, carrying 126 guns and a crew of 850 men (Glete 1999: 17ff; Zettersten 1903: 574). *Kronan* constituted a floating society, both in terms of the number of crew and its social structure (Einarsson 1997: 212).

Kronan was discovered by Anders Franzén in August 1980, off the southeast coast of Öland. Three engineers, Sten Ahlberg, Bengt Börjesson and Bengt Grisell, assisted Franzén, who was celebrated for his earlier discovery of *Vasa*. In 1981 Kalmar County Museum began the marine archaeological investigations of *Kronan.* Hitherto more than 30,000 objects have been recovered from the site during 30 years of continuous underwater investigations (Einarsson 2010: 3ff).

The wreck of *Kronan* is in archaeological terms a closed find, meaning that it forms an entity that reached a given place at a single moment in time. Because such a find has a precise context, it can yield far more information than can many separate finds made in different places. A shipwreck often represents an unconditional deposition of historical information, since no one has time to carefully, purposefully sift through what should be saved for posterity, and thus to affect the image presented of the era.

The site of the wreck of *Kronan* lies 6 km east of the village of Hulterstad, in southeastern Öland, at a depth of 26 m (Einarsson 2001: 20ff). The seabed is a thin layer of sand over a thick layer of glacial and moraine clay that protects any organic or inorganic object embedded in it. Because of the low salt concentration no presence of marine wood boring organisms such as *Teredo navalis* have been observed on the site.

What has survived of *Kronan* is mainly the coherent two-thirds of the port side of her hull, from the stern forward (**Fig. 2.8**). The hull is entirely built of oak, while parts of the interior structure like bulkheads and deck planking (orlop) may be of pine. No remains of the rigging, which presumably would have been made of pine and spruce, have been recovered so far.

The hull structure is broken forward of the main mast-step. Consequently the bow including the fo'c's'le is missing, representing approximately one-third of the ship's length. The remaining coherent hull structure measures 40 m x 20 m. It has lain flat on the seabed since shortly after *Kronan* sank. On the inner side of the surviving part of the hull lay thousands of artefacts in tightly compacted sediments. The arrangement

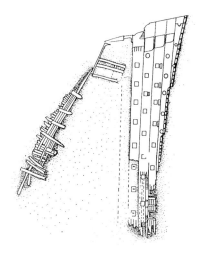

Fig. 2.8. *Site plan of* Kronan *(drawing: L. Einarsson).*

of *Kronan*'s seven decks was, from the upper-most at the stern: the 10 m-long poop-deck; below it the roughly 20 m-long quarter-deck; and then, in turn, the upper-, middle- and lower-decks, the orlop, and the hold.

In the western part of the site, the lowest part of *Kronan*'s starboard side protrudes 1-2 m above the seabed; the upper part of the side was shattered by the explosion when she sank. To the south, where the hull broke apart, its forepart is missing. To the north, the massive stern protrudes some 4 m above the seabed. The size of the timbers ranges from fragments up to sturdy structural elements like the sternpost, measuring nearly 2 m in circumference. The deepest part of the coherent hull structure rests 1.5 m below the seabed.

Hardly anything of the athwart-ship structure remains in its original position. Deck beams and deck planks have collapsed on top of the ceiling planking. Three factors explain how *Kronan* has broken up: the explosion after which she sank; subsequent natural processes like wave energy, erosion by currents, and shifting sands; and human interference from fishing, mine-sweeping equipment and archaeology.

A study of the preserved wreck structure on the site may, however, reveal a number of factors favourable for ship preservation. The fast sinking that succeeded the explosion, the considerable weight of the remaining contents of the ship, in particular the ordnance, probably compressed larger elements of the wreck into the protective sediments on the site shortly after the sinking. The starboard side of the hull constitutes a wall protecting the centre of the site, where the vast majority of the artefacts are deposited. Wooden sculpture that had originally been fastened by iron nails onto the ceiling planking on the port side of the upper deck was discovered *in situ* despite its shallow position within the sediments. The carvings had clearly been protected from erosion by structural elements such as knees and stringers (Einarsson 1990: 285).

A separate part of the hull structure measuring about 8 m x 22 m (**Fig. 2.9**), possibly from the starboard side, is located about 35 m south-west of the main wreck site. This section may have been connected with the main wreck for a considerable period of time after *Kronan* sank, thus contributing to the protection of the interior of the wreck from degradation.

Data collected from the site over the years have shown that the ship came to rest on the seabed at an angle of about 45° from vertical. The forward third section of the ship had broken off as a result of the explosion. After a short period of time, the upper part of the port side from the lower deck collapsed, causing a longitudinal fracture of that side. The fracture is visible at several locations inside the wreck, particularly close to the stern. Hitherto, no actual separation of the upper and lower part of the port side has been observed. The fact that the upper part of the port side came to rest flat on the seabed meant that large quantities of the external embellishment were embedded safely in the anaerobic clay beneath the ship's side. Test trenches have confirmed this (Einarsson 1994: 13ff).

Visibility around the wreck is excellent – at best about 25 m – due to the off-shore location and the general absence of human pollution and algae. The light-reflecting sandy seabed contributes to the excellent visibility as well.

Fig. 2.9. Detail of the sculpture preserved on Kronan *(photo: L. Einarsson).*

When analysing the conditions for preservation of the wreck it is important to study the nature of the sailing vessel: how it was built and of what material. Also the extent of loss and damage of the hull structure in connection with the explosion and opening of the ship is of great relevance to assess. The qualities of the anaerobic sediments for preservation on the site, but also the negative effects of natural erosion, are factors to be considered. Questions regarding human interference in connection with gun salvage operations on the site in the 17th century, as well as modern underwater archaeological investigations, are also activities that have had a considerable impact on the wreck.

Chemical analyses of isolated oak planks from *Kronan* indicate less presence of iron compared to *Vasa*, but a higher amount of organically-bound sulphur, which is relatively stable (Sandström 2003). However, further analyses of a large amount of representative material from the wreck are necessary in order to draw general conclusions regarding the degradation of the wood.

The aim of the remaining marine archaeological work on *Kronan* falls into three successive phases: 1) A complete investigation and recovery of the hull area. About 85% of this phase has been completed by 2011; 2) A marine archaeological documentation of the uncovered hull structure. This is planned to begin immediately after the first phase is completed, and includes analysing and interpreting *Kronan*'s ability to sail and manoeuvre, and placing her in a technical-historical perspective; 3) To recover the port side of the hull. The archaeological motive for recovering the port side is the possibility this offers of restoring the external sculptures discovered underneath to their original places on the hull. If Phase 3 is not feasible, the investigation would be concluded by covering the wreck with a protective layer of sand.

References

Einarsson, L., 1990. *Kronan – underwater archaeological investigations of a 17th century man-of-war. The nature, aims and development of a maritime cultural project. International Journal of Nautical Archaeology* 19.4: 279-297.
Einarsson, L., 1994. *Rapport om 1994 års marinarkeologiska undersökningar av vraket efter regalskeppet Kronan* (Kalmar, Kalmar County Museum).
Einarsson, L., 1997. Artefacts from the *Kronan* (1676): categories, preservation and social structure. In: M. Redknap (ed.), *Artefacts from Wrecks* (Oxford, Oxbow): 209-218.
Einarsson, L., 2001. *Kronan* (Kalmar, Kalmar County Museum).
Einarsson, L., 2009. *Rapport om 2009 års marinarkeologiska undersökningar av vraket efter regalskeppet Kronan* (Kalmar, Kalmar County Museum).
Glete, J., 1999. Hur stor var Kronan? Något om stora örlogsskepp i Europa under 1600-talets senare hälft. *Forum Navale* 55: 17-25.
Sandström, M., 2003. *The Kronan. XANAS of of oak surface. Report on isolated analysis of oak plank from Kronan* (Stockholm, Stockholm University).
Zettersten, A., 1903. *Svenska Flottans Historia. Åren 1635-1680* (Stockholm, J. Seligmann).

2.2.5 Stinesminde: a well-preserved 17th-century wreck from Mariager Fjord, Denmark

David Gregory & Jørgen Dencker

In 1987 the National Museum of Denmark led a collaborative investigation of a well-preserved wreck that lay in 12 m of water in Mariager Fjord. Mariager Fjord lies on the east coast of Jutland, Denmark, and opens into the Kattegat. The wreck lies about 600 m south-west of the fishing village Stinesminde, on the north side of the fjord, and has colloquially become known as the "Stindesminde wreck".

The archaeological investigations show that the ship was a trading vessel, 20 m long, 5.9 m wide and 2.7 m deep. It was of Lübeck origin and radiocarbon dated to 1640 (+/- 50 years). The ship appears to have been emptied of cargo and had probably been laid up prior to sinking. It was flush built with strong wales, relatively pointed at the bow and rounded at the stern (**Figs. 2.10 & 2.11**). Parts of the captain's cabin survived, the rudder was still standing behind the stern and the tiller was also preserved. In front of the cabin, the ship's pump and a large windlass were found. The ship was preserved up to the main deck and three loading hatches were found. The ship had one or possibly two masts with the main-mast still in its original position in the middle of the ship, preserved to a height of almost 2 m above the deck's surface.

The environment of the wreck site, devoid of shipworm intrusion, has made it possible to preserve one of the best examples of early 17th-century shipbuilding found in Danish waters. Following the archaeological in-

Fig. 2.10. The Stinesminde wreck (drawing: Thorkild Thomasen).

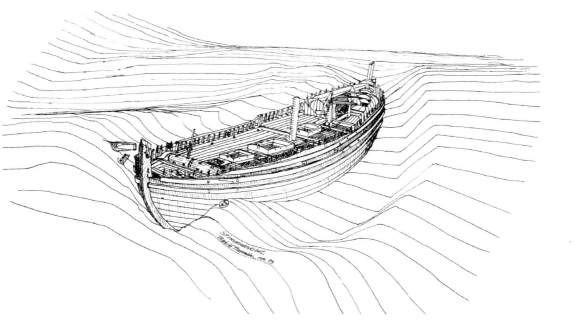

vestigations of the 1980s, there was great interest to raise the wreck. Even then, the capacity and funds to raise, conserve and display the find were not available. To the dismay of locals, it was decided to leave the wreck where it was and protect it. However, even though the site was not under threat from shipworm, it was very attractive for sports diving and there was a need for protection against this. At the end of the investigations in 1989, a large fine-meshed net was placed over the site to prevent divers from accessing the inner parts of the wreck. In 2004 the site was revisited and the net was still shown to be effective, having now an added layer of protection due to colonising mussels. However, it had been cut in several places in order to gain access to the inner parts of the wreck. After this discovery, the site was covered with sediment and the net was repaired.

Fig. 2.11. Detail of the Stinesminde wreck's bow (photo: Svend Erik Jørgensen). (See also the photo on the front cover of this book.)

References

Frederiksen, J., & Skriver, C., 2004. *FHM 4427/4, Stinesmindevraget. Rapport vedr. besigtigelse af Stinesmindevraget* (Århus, Moesgård Museum).
Rieck, F., 1993. A Baltic Coastal Vessel – Latest Research on the wreck of a 17th century Merchant Ship at Stinesminde, Mariager Fjord, Denmark. *VIII International Baltic Seminar, 5.-7. July 1990* (Kotka, Provincial Museum of Kymenlaakso): 137-144.

2.2.6 The Kolding cog

David Gregory

Fig. 2.12. The floor timbers and part of the mast-step of the cog that has been exposed and extensively attacked by shipworm (photo: David Robinson, © National Museum of Denmark).

In 1943 a shipwreck was found in Kolding's inner fjord, which was identified to be a cog, a ship-type commonly used between the 11th and 14th centuries. The ship was investigated by the National Museum of Denmark and the Danish Maritime Museum. After the initial investigations the majority of the wreck remained on the bottom of the fjord but loose timbers were raised and deposited for storage in an iron barge sunk at the mouth of Kolding Stream. This is the stream that flows through Kolding and into the fjord. The hope was that following World War II it would be possible to re-investigate the site and conserve the raised timbers. Following several attempts to relocate the wreck in the fjord in the 1960s and 1970s, it was not until the late 1990s that the wreck site was eventually relocated. The

wreck's remains, the very bottom of the hull, were approximately 15 m long and 5 m wide and were built of European white oak. It lay in 3 m of water and, at the time of its re-discovery, was lying largely exposed on the bottom with those timbers protruding above the seabed having been heavily attacked by shipworm (**Fig. 2.12**).

These timbers had been exposed to the seawater for a long time and upon examination there were no signs of living shipworm. The lengths of some of the tunnels were 40-50 cm with a diameter of ca. 5 mm. Interestingly, many of the abandoned tunnels had provided a home for ragworms (*Nereididae*). Concerning the post-depositional formation processes of the wreck site, it is hypothesised that the ship settled into the sediment and those parts which were exposed, from the inside of the turn of the bilge, have at some point since the wrecking been attacked by shipworm. This has led to a weakening of the upper parts of the ship, which broke off and subsequently were washed away, or, having become waterlogged, were deposited near the wreck.

The initial plan was for the wreck to be raised, along with the timbers stored in the stream, and documented in full-scale in order to gain more information about the ship's construction (**Fig. 2.13**). The timbers were to be re-buried in the fjord rather than conserved. However, the local museum expressed an interest to conserve and exhibit the timbers. The fate of the cog is currently uncertain as 10 years after excavation and raising, the timbers currently lie in fresh water holding tanks awaiting conservation.

Fig. 2.13. Three-dimensional reconstruction of the excavated remains of the Kolding cog (drawing: Fred Hocker, © National Museum of Denmark).

References

Hocker, F., 2000. Relocating the Kolding cog. *Maritime Archaeology Newsletter from Roskilde, Denmark* 14: 50-55.

3. Other European waters

3.1 The North Sea and Wadden Sea
Martijn Manders

The North Sea and Wadden Sea are situated just outside of the Baltic Sea, on the west side of the Skagerrak. The salinity here is much higher than in the Baltic, approximately 34 to 37 practical salinity units (psu), which equates to approximately 3.4-3.7%. This means that the shipworm species, *Teredo navalis*, is already active here and this has been known to be the case for around 500 years.

The dynamics of the seabed (tidal change, changing gulleys, waves and swell) are a blessing as well as a curse for underwater cultural heritage: ships that sink are often covered with sediment in a short period of time, thus leaving them protected against the attack of shipworms. However, the dynamic nature of the marine environment can also lead to the wrecks' re-exposure. What can be observed is that wrecks are being attacked and deteriorated cyclically over time, sometimes with intervals of centuries. Every time wood is exposed, parts of the wreck are destroyed before the wreck is hopefully covered again (**Fig. 3.1**).

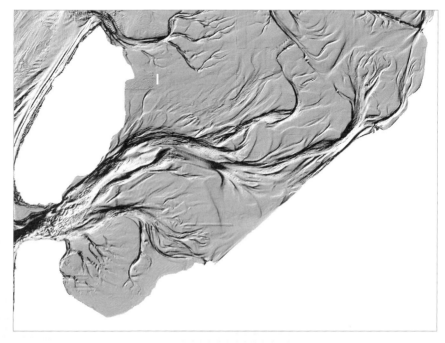

Fig. 3.1. The Wadden Sea. This picture is the result of thousands of depth measurements. It clearly shows the gulleys that have a strong erosive effect on the shipwrecks (image courtesy RWS).

In the Wadden Sea, due to the 1932 building of the Afsluitdijk (a dyke across the former Zuiderzee), this pattern of sedimentation and erosion has been disturbed. As a result, in the southern Dutch part of the sea, the seabed is eroding very quickly.

An example of a site under threat is the BZN 10 wreck, discovered in 1999. This 17th-century trader, probably of German origin, was carrying a cargo of Iberian jars, grapes and schist slates. Only a few deck beams, remains of cargo, and cannon were protruding from the seabed when the wreck was first found (**Fig. 3.2**). The starboard side of the ship remained well preserved with the port side eroded away. After a short significance assessment in 2000, the site was covered in several phases (2000, 2001 and 2003) with polypropylene nets in order to preserve it *in situ*. Due to the dynamics of the area in combination with the continuous attack of *Teredo navalis*, the wreck (which can be almost reconstructed completely) is considered to be well preserved.

Fig. 3.2. *A pine wood deck beam of the BZN 10 wreck, heavily attacked by* Teredo navalis *(photo courtesy RCE).*

This is a much different scenario from the Baltic Sea and again highlights the value of that area as a resource for European and world-wide maritime history. All the protruding wood of BZN 10 has been attacked by shipworms. Degradation of the site has been a continuous process ever since the first parts of the vessel were exposed. Pieces of wood weakened from shipworm attacks have been broken off by strong currents as well as by fishing nets. The physical protection that has been applied will prevent or slow down the deterioration processes for a while. The overall area, however, is under constant threat, and it is predicted that the unstable seabed will erode for at least another few metres in the coming decades (**Fig. 3.3**). Thus, even the current attempts at preserving the site *in situ* may be in vain. Such measures, however, give us some time to decide what to do.

Fig. 3.3. Four wrecks in the Wadden Sea: BZN 3, 8, 10 and 11. The first three are physically protected. This picture shows the difference between 2003 and 2004, showing the effect of the in-situ protection (red is sedimentation) and the eroding seabed around it (blue is erosion area) (image courtesy RWS).

References

Huisman, D.J., Manders, M.R., Kretschmar, E., Klaassen, R.K.W.M., & Lamersdorf, N., 2008. Burial conditions and wood degradation on archaeological sites in the Netherlands. *International Biodeterioration and Biodegradation* 61: 33-44.

Manders, M., 2010. Multibeam recording as a way to monitor shipwreck sites. In: M. Manders et al. (eds.), *MACHU Final report Nr. 3* (RCE Amersfoort): 59-66.

Manders, M.R., 2006. The in situ protection of a 17[th]century trading vessel in the Netherlands. In: R. Grenier, D. Nutley & I. Cochran (eds), *Heritage at Risk, Special Issue: Underwater Cultural Heritage at Risk. Managing Natural and Human Impacts* (Paris, ICOMOS): 70-72.

3.2 The Mediterranean – a contrast to the Baltic case studies
Giulia Boetto

The Mediterranean Sea preserves a valuable and vast archaeological and historical heritage that is shared by 21 countries. It is very hard to estimate the number of shipwrecks in this marine environment, which covers an approximate area of 2.5 million km².

In the Mediterranean, Parker (1992) recorded 1,189 shipwrecks up to AD 1500. His list is far from complete: several countries are under-represented due to a lack of information and research. The number of shipwrecks is of course higher than Parker's catalogue. If we just consider the French Mediterranean Territorial Waters and Contiguous Zone (60,213 km²), DRASSM (*Département des recherches archéologiques subaquatiques et sous-marines*) has recorded 3,000 underwater archaeological sites and estimates that there are up to 2,000 shipwrecks (ranging from antiquity to modern times). Moreover, the number of shipwrecks could be greater (up to 5,000) if the marine area protected by French legislation could be extended in the future to the Exclusive Economic Zone (110,407 km²).[1]

In the warm and temperate waters of the Mediterranean Sea, exposed timbers can be seriously damaged and finally very quickly decomposed due to the high activity of wood borers and fungi (Pournou et al. 1998: 61). A variety of complex processes influence the dynamics of transformation of a sunken ship into a shipwreck. Frequently, in the Mediterranean these processes make wooden structures completely disappear (Gianfrotta & Pomey 1981; Beltrame 2002). Nevertheless, when covered by an imperishable cargo or by a fixed layer of sediments, large sections of wooden shipwrecks can be very well preserved, providing an extraordinary resource for archaeological and historical research.

It is obvious that in this marine environment, wooden timbers cannot be left uncovered on the seabed because they will rapidly deteriorate. At the end of an archaeological survey, the reburial of excavated wooden timbers with sand is the most common *in-situ* protection system that is today largely adopted in the Mediterranean. This is, without doubt, the most economic method as being efficient and easy to implement if the wreck lies on a sandy surface in relatively shallow waters. This method is coupled, especially in the last few years, with the use of geotextiles. However, these systems need to be supplemented by continuous supervision to observe and ensure long-term preservation. It is imperative that wood does not re-emerge from the seabed and become exposed to biodeteriogenic attacks or to clandestine looters.

A large number of examples show that wood, left unprotected, disappears, as it is destroyed by marine borers. Pomey (1998) published an interesting contribution concerning this topic. From 1991 to 1998, off the French coasts, 26 Roman shipwrecks that had been excavated and

1. If we also consider the internal waterways, the number of underwater sites connected with coastal infrastructure increases exponentially (up to 8,000). Source: DRASSM (Ministry of Culture and Communication) – National Archaeological Inventory.

Fig. 3.4. Port-Vendres
3 shipwreck in 1989
(photo: D. Colls,
courtesy DRASSM,
Marseille).

Fig. 3.4. Port-Vendres 3 shipwreck in 1989 (photo: D. Colls, courtesy DRASSM, Marseille).

then reburied with sand from the seabed about 30 years before were re-examined within the framework of a research project on dendrochronology. In 35% of the shipwrecks, mainly at about 30 m in depth, the wood was found to be in very good condition because the layer of sand hadn't moved over the years thanks to the depth and to the natural conditions at the sites. In 46% of the shipwrecks, the wooden timber had almost completely disintegrated, while in 19% of the cases, wood was found in a poor and fragile condition. One of the main causes of this situation, which occurred mainly with shipwrecks resting in shallow waters, was the result of anthropogenic intrusion that altered the fragile equilibrium reached with the reburial of the shipwrecks.

The example of the shallow water shipwrecks discovered in Laurons Bay is very instructive. In 1994, four of the six ancient shipwrecks discovered here were more or less completely destroyed, mostly as a result of scavenging by wreck-hunters, vandals and swimmers (Pomey 1998). Only the shipwrecks Laurons 1 and Laurons 2 were found well protected and still intact. The latter is well known to nautical archaeologists as, at the time of excavation in 1980, this shipwreck preserved the only archaeological data available for the reconstruction of the deck, rail and steering system of a sea-going Roman cargo vessel. Only a few fragments of timbers, planking and ceiling were left of the Laurons 3, 4, 5 and 6 shipwrecks. The Laurons 3 and 4 shipwrecks were well preserved when discovered in 1977 and after three excavation campaigns in the 1980s.

The same thing occurred to the Roman shipwreck Port Vendres 3 resting at a depth of 6 m (mid-3rd century AD, Pyrénées-Orientales). In 1989,

seven planks and eight frames constituted the remains of the shipwreck (**Fig. 3.4**). In 2005-2006, the site was re-opened and the wood re-studied (Jézégou 2007: 632). Unfortunately, the timbers, covered after the first campaign with a layer of very mobile gravel-sand, were found to be in poor condition, and partially destroyed by marine action and biological attacks (**Fig. 3.5**).

Fig. 3.5. Port-Vendres 3 shipwreck in 2005 (photo: M.-P. Jézégou, DRASSM, Marseille).

Slabs of cement, metallic panels and electrically welded galvanized wire netting has been also used together with sandbags, layers of sand and geotextile to protect hulls from anthropogenic intrusions (looters and trawler fishing nets), from destructive marine action (waves, storms) and from biodeteriogenic decay. In Italy (Davidde 2004) and Spain (Phoenician Mazarron 1 & 2 shipwrecks; Neguerela 2000: 193-194), these protection systems proved their efficacy. Beside this, sophisticated projects for *in-situ* protection of wooden shipwrecks have been also elaborate, and never been completed due to lack of a broad archaeological survey on the ship-wrecks themselves (Bonaiuti 2004).

Few examples from Italy (D'Urbano et al. 1989; Bettazzi et al. 2003; Macchioni 2004; Bartolini et al. 2004), Greece (Pournou et al. 1998) and Croatia (Pournou 2010) show the study of the degree of conservation of waterlogged wooden timbers by mean of biological and/or physical analyses. Moreover, the post-medieval Zakynthos shipwreck in Greece provided the first, and until now unique, opportunity to test the efficacy of different grades of the geotextile "Terram" for *in-situ* protection of a Mediterranean wreck (Pournou et al. 1998).

Finally, in Mediterranean countries the discussion to preserve hull remains *in situ* is today at its beginning and surely will progress in the future as this archaeological and historical heritage needs to be preserved in a viable and efficient way for future researchers. However, it is regrettable that some Mediterranean governments attach more importance to setting up very expensive and time-consuming protection systems than to setting up research programmes designed to gather high-level scientific information from shipwrecks deemed of archaeological and historical significance.

Acknowledgements

The author would like to thank Frédéric Leroy (DRASSM, Marseille) for his help concerning the French inventory of cultural heritage; Marie-Pierre Jézégou (DRASSM, Marseille) for sharing her data about the Port-Vendres 3 shipwreck; and, finally, Carlos De Juan (University of Valencia) for some bibliographical references and general information concerning Spain.

References

Bartolini, M., Capretti, C., Galotta, G., Giachi, G., Macchioni, N., Nugari, M.P., & Pizzo, B., 2004. Il porto di Neapolis: indagini diagnostiche. *Archaeologia Maritima Mediterranea* 1: 82-91.

Beltrame, C., 2002. Investigating Processes of Wreck Formation: Wrecks on the Beach Environment in the Mediterranean Sea. *Archeologia subacquea. Studi, ricerche e documenti* III: 381-398.

Bettazzi, F., Giachi, G., Staccioli, G., & Chimichi, S., 2003. Chemical characterisation of wood of Roman ships brought to light in the recently discovered ancient harbour of Pisa (Tuscany, Italy). *Holzforschung* 57.4: 373-376.

Bonaiuti, R., 2004. Progetto di conservazione in situ del relitto romano di Procchio. *Archaeologia Maritima Mediterranea* 1: 151-156.

Davidde, B., 2004. Methods and strategies for the conservation and museum display in situ of underwater cultural heritage. *Archaeologia Maritima Mediterranea* 1: 137-150.

D'Urbano, S., Meucci, C., Nugari, M.P., & Priori, G.F., 1989. Valutazione del degrado biologico e chimico di legni archeologici in ambiente marino. In: G. Tampone (ed.), *Il Restauro del Legno,* Vol. 1 (Florence, Nardini): 79-84.

Gianfrotta, P.A., & Pomey, P., 1981. *Archeologia subacquea: storia, tecniche, scoperte e relitti* (Milan, Arnoldo Mondadori).

Jézégou, M.-P., 2007. Découvertes sous-marines le long du littoral des Pyrénées-Orientales. In: J. Kotarba, G. Castellvi, & Fl. Mazière (eds.), *Carte Archeologique de la Gaule, Les Pyrénées-Orientales,* 66 (Paris, Académie des Inscriptions et Belles-Lettres): 622-642.

Macchioni, N., 2003. Physical characteristics of the wood from the excavations of the ancient port of Pisa. *Journal of Cultural Heritage* 4: 85-89.

Neguerela, I., 2000. Managing the maritime heritage: the National Maritime Archaeological Museum and National Centre for Underwater Research, Cartagena, Spain. *International Jounal of Nautical Archaeology* 29.2 : 179-198.

Parker, A.J., 1992. *Ancient shipwrecks of the Mediterranean & the Roman Provinces* (Oxford, Archaeopress).

Pomey, P., 1998. Remarques sur la conservation "in situ" du bois de quelques épaves antiques de Méditérranée. In: C. Bonnot-Diconne, X. Hiron, Q. Khôi Tran & P. Hoffman (eds.), *Proceedings of the 7th ICOM-CC Working Group, Wet Organic Archaeological Materials Conference, Grenoble 1998* (Grenoble, Arc-Nucléart): 53-57.

Pournou, A., Jones, A.M., & Moss, T., 1998. In situ Protection of the Zakynthos Wreck. In: C. Bonnot-Diconne, X. Hiron, Q. Khôi Tran & P. Hoffman (eds), *Proceedings of the 7th ICOM-CC Working Group, Wet Organic Archaeological Materials Conference, Grenoble 1998* (Grenoble, Arc-Nucléart): 58-64.

Pournou, A., 2010. *The Preservation State of Waterlogged Wood from a Roman Shipwreck at Pag island, Croatia* (Athens, unpublished report).

4. The Baltic Sea environment

Zyad Al Hamdani & Christin Appelqvist

4.1 Introduction

The Baltic Sea is one of the largest bodies of brackish water in the world; it lies approximately between latitude 53°N to 63°N and longitude 10°E to 26°E and has an area of ca. 377,000 km² (415,000 km² including the Kattegat) (**Fig. 4.1**).

The Baltic Sea drains an area of 1.6×10^6 km² and has an annual freshwater input (including precipitation) of 660 km³. The annual discharge of

Fig. 4.1. The Baltic Sea (image: Jeff Schmaltz, MODIS Rapid Response Team, NASA/GSFC).

brackish water is 950 km³ while the inflow of saline bottom water is estimated to be 475 km³/year. This brackish water body is not very deep
(**Fig. 4.2**): the deepest point is ca. 459 m below sea level (BSL), which is
situated about 70 km south/south-west of Stockholm. The southern part
of the Baltic Sea has a depth range of 25-75 m; in the central part the
depth ranges from 100-200 m while in the northern part it is about 50-100
m deep. There are nine countries surrounding the Baltic Sea with a total
population of ca. 85 million; 15 million live within 10 km of the coast and
29 million within 50 km of the coast.

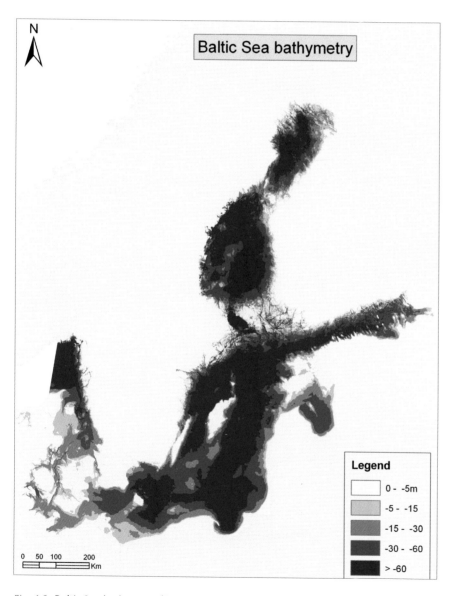

Fig. 4.2. Baltic Sea bathymetry (BALANCE project, Al Hamdani et al. 2007).

4.2 The geological history

From a geological perspective, the Baltic Sea is very young. The Baltic went through different stages during its history of formation since the Eemian Sea at about 130,000-115,000 BP (years before present). Nevertheless, its creation only started after the last glacial retreat 17,000-15,000 BP (Erikkson 2009). An almost 3 km-thick ice sheet covered a major part of Scandinavia until it started to melt due to global warming. The factors that determine the characteristics of the de-glaciation period of the Baltic Sea formation is the submergence and emergence of the region due to the weight of the ice and subsequent isostatic readjustment of its height (isostatic and eustatic effects), and the connecting channels it could find to the North Sea through the Great Belt of Denmark or through what are now the large lakes of Sweden. The development of the Baltic Sea is described by the following stages:

About 18,000 BP, and after the maximum extension in the Jutland Main Border Line, the glacial retreat followed the west coast of Sweden (**Fig. 4.3**), covering Zealand and extending south-west to reach the Belts.

The ice margin retreated to the Sound and the western part of Skåne in Sweden at about 16,000 BP, but it still covered the southern part of Zealand and followed the present southern coast of the Baltic Sea (**Fig. 4.4**). The ice margin was directly connected to the Kattegat marine basin by a broad melt-water channel.

Fig. 4.3. The Baltic at about 18,000 BP (Jensen et al. 2002).

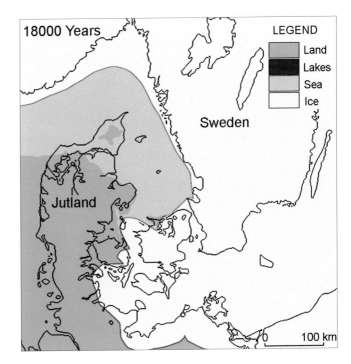

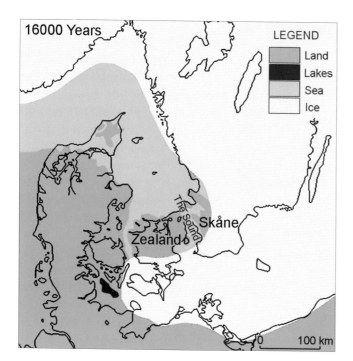

Fig. 4.4. The Baltic at about 16,000 BP (Jensen et al. 2002).

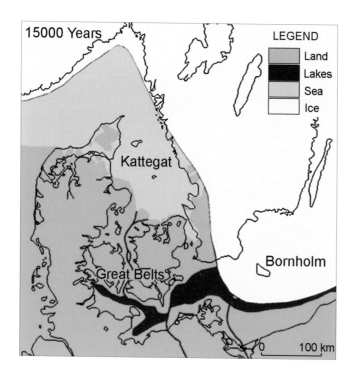

Fig. 4.5. The Baltic at about 15,000 BP (Jensen et al. 2002).

The ice margin retreated even further by 15,000 BP to reach the middle of Skåne and the west of Bornholm. A large lake had been dammed in front of the ice margin with connection through the Great Belt to the Kattegat (**Fig. 4.5**) (Jensen et al. 2002).

The first stage in the evolution of the Baltic Sea is called the Baltic Ice Lake (BIL). Glacial melt-water accumulated in front of the ice sheet (Kallio 2006). The lake was bounded to the north by the front of the retreating ice sheet while the Billingen bedrock ridge in south-central Sweden formed a "wall" between the sea in the west and the dammed BIL to the east (Andrén 2003a). The BIL existed from 13,000 BP to 11,600 BP, successively increasing its area as the Scandinavian ice sheet melted (**Fig. 4.6**). At the end of the BIL phase the melting ice opened a route to the Kattegat where eustatic sea level rise exceeded the isostatic uplift in the central part of Sweden causing the inflow of the North Sea saline waters. The lake level decreased by about 25 m (Jensen et al. 2002).

About 11,500 BP a strait was established through the central part of Sweden just south of the ice sheet margin and the BIL basin was transformed into a brackish basin called the Yolida Sea (**Fig. 4.7**) (Andrén 2003b). This name was taken from a mussel (*Yolida arctica*) that inhabited the sea at that time. The sea surface level during the Yolida Sea formation (11,600-10,700 BP) reached to ca. 35 m below present-day level (Jensen et al. 2002). In the southern Bal-

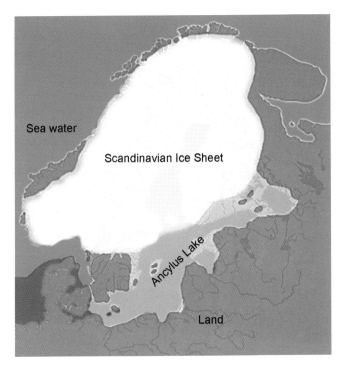

Fig. 4.6. Baltic Ice Lake, 11,700-11,600 BP (Andrén 2003a).

Fig. 4.7. The Yolida Sea, 11,600-10,700 BP (Andrén 2003b).

tic region and around Denmark. In the northern part of the sea, large areas of Sweden and Finland were exposed under the retreating ice but still were under water (Kallio 2006).

The isostatic uplift in the central part of Sweden caused the straits that linked the Baltic Sea to the ocean to close, and the Ancylus Lake phase (10,700-9,000 BP) of the post-glacial Baltic began (**Fig. 4.8**). The Ancylus Lake is named after a freshwater mollusc (*Ancylus fluviatilis*) which lives in shoreline zones of large lakes. Earlier in the late Ancylus Lake stage damming caused the water level to rise, causing the inundation of extensive areas of land along the south coast of the Baltic where no significant land uplift took place. However, the land uplift near the Gulf of Bothnia exceeded the sea level rise creating new land during the transgression period.

At the end of the Ancylus Lake stage (at about 10,000 BP) the water level in the lake decreased within a few hundred years, causing a gradual drainage through the Great Belt of Denmark which was manifested by calm lake and estuarine sedimentation followed by a gradual change into brackish conditions at about 9,100 BP. A complete marine environment was reached in the Great Belt at about 8,400 BP (Jensen et al. 2002).

There was a short transition period between the Ancylus Lake phase and the establishment of the Littorina Sea. Called the Mastogloia Sea period, it existed from 8,400 BP until about 8,200 BP. The

Fig. 4.8. The Ancylus Lake, 10,700-9,000 BP (Andrén 2003c).

Fig. 4.9. The Littorina Sea, 8,400-8,200 BP (Andrén 2004).

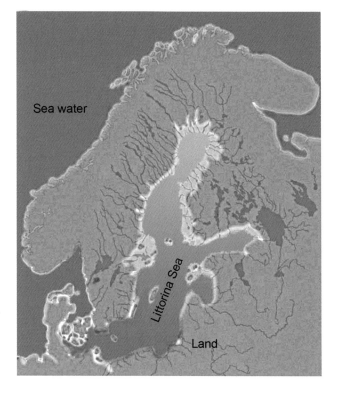

name comes from a diatom that lives in semi-brackish waters. The Littorina Sea was the beginning of brackish-marine waters of the Baltic; the name comes from the marine gastropod *Littoria littoria*. In this stage an influx of saline waters started to take place through the Great Belt at about 8,400 BP (**Fig. 4.9**). More and more saline water entered the Baltic basin as the connecting channels of the Great Belt became broader and by 7,500 BP the Littorina Sea had reached the south coast of Finland. The eustatic sea level rise in ocean level led to transgression at the early stages of the Littorina Sea. As a result, water level along the southeastern coast of Finland rose by a few metres (Kallio 2006). In the southern Littorina Sea, the sea level rise was faster and reached a level of 2-3 m below that of present. When sea level rise ended between 6,000-5,000 BP, the transgressive phase of the Littorina Sea was also finished. Since that time the Littorina Sea has continued to develop gradually up to the present and new land has been added to the coast of Finland at a steadily declining rate (Tikkanen & Oksanen 2002).

The relative sea level fluctuation curve for the southern Baltic Sea near the Polish coast is shown in **Fig. 4.10** (Uścinowicz 2006).

4.3 The Baltic Sea's physical characteristics

The Baltic Sea has a complicated hydrographical system with a complex bathymetry. It is a highly dynamic sea that is strongly influenced by atmospheric circulation, hydro-geological processes and restricted water exchange due to its narrow entrance area. The Baltic Sea is divided into six basins with a number of sub-basins: 1) the Baltic Proper including the sill area at the entrance, Arkona Basin, Bornholm Basin, western and eastern Gotland Basin, Gdansk Deep, Northern Baltic Proper; 2) the Gulf of Bothnia, including Bothnian Bay and Bothnian Sea; 3) the Gulf of Finland; 4) the Gulf of Riga; 5) the Danish Straits, including the Belts; and 6) the Kattegat (**Fig. 4.11**) (Omstedt et al. 2004a).

These basins differ in size, volume, ice cover, temperature, salinity, and residence time of water (**Fig. 4.12**; **Table 4.1**). The Kattegat has a surface salinity of 20-25 psu (practical salinity unit), the Baltic Proper has a salinity range of 6-8 psu while in the north and in the northeastern parts of the Baltic the salinity drops to below 1 psu (HELCOM 2009). This low salinity and brackish nature of the Baltic Sea influences the number and occurrence of natural species in different parts of the Baltic. The maximum number of species is found at salinities greater than 30 psu; nevertheless, at salinities below 8 the number of species increases as some freshwater species can survive in such an environment.

The Baltic Sea has the unique property of vertical stratification of the water mass. Stratification is caused by difference in salinity between the surface and the bottom water layer and difference in water temperature

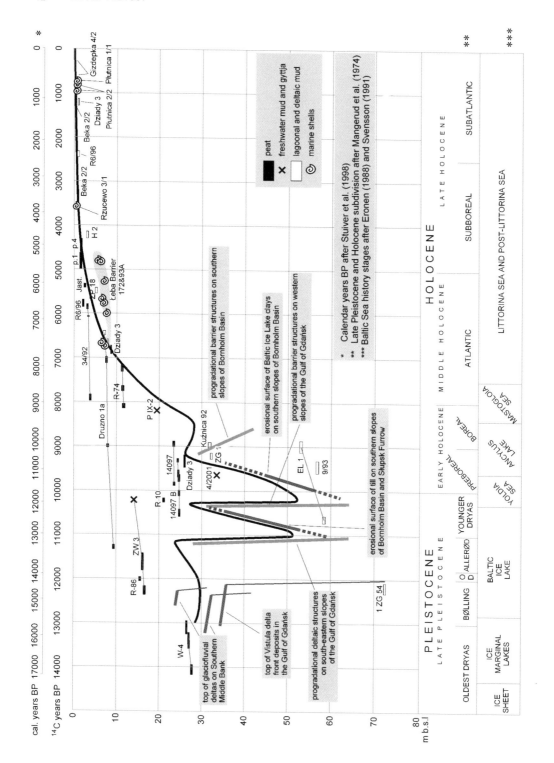

Fig. 4.10. Relative sea level changes for the southern Baltic Sea (Uścinowicz 2006).

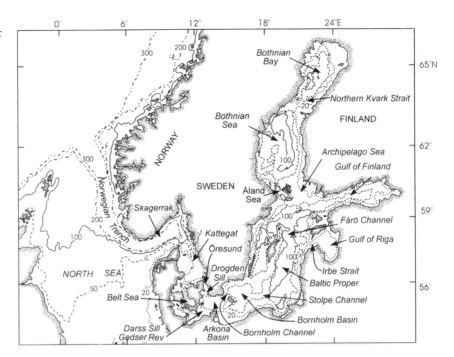

Fig. 4.11. The Baltic Sea's major basins and the Kattegat (Omstedt et al. 2004a).

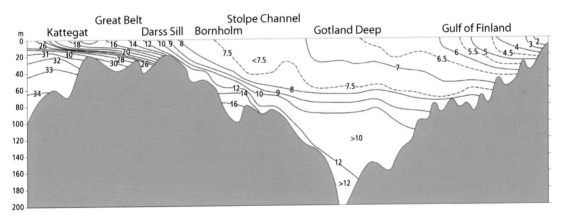

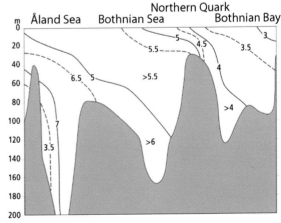

Fig. 4.12. The panel above shows a transect of the Baltic Sea from the Kattegat through the Danish Straits and the Baltic proper into the Gulf of Finland. The panel to the right shows a transect from the Åland Sea, the Bothnian Sea through Northern Quark into Bothnian Bay (HELCOM 2009; Leppäranta & Myrberg 2008). The isohaline represents the salinity values at different geographic locations and different depths.

Table 4.1. *Physical characteristics of the Baltic Sea, Kattegat, and Skagerrak (Al Hamdani & Reker 2007).*

Sub-area	Area	Volume	Salinity range	Max. depth	Ave. depth
	km²	km³	psu	m	m
1. Baltic Proper	211,069	13,045	5-10	459	62.1
2. Gulf of Bothnia	115,516	6,389	0-7	230	60.2
3. Gulf of Finland	29,600	1,100	0-7	123	38.0
4. Gulf of Riga	16,330	424	6-10	> 60	26.0
5. Danish Straits & Kattegat	42,408	802	8-32	109	18.9
Total Baltic Sea	415,266	21,721	0-32	459	52.3
Total HELCOM region	409,828[1]	-	-	-	-
Total Skagerrak	-	-	32-33	725	-

from one season to another. The effect of stratification on oxygen content is significant; it prevents ventilation and oxygenation of the bottom water layers and sediments by reducing vertical mixing which can result in oxygen depletion.

The water column of the central Baltic proper is permanently stratified despite its shallow depth (ca. 55 m). The position of the permanent halocline changes from season to season is shown in **Fig. 4.13**.

The Baltic Sea's oceanographic conditions and its circulation system are strongly influenced by bathymetry, the narrow straits that connect the basins, and the presence of shallow sills at its entrance, such as the Drogden sill in the Sound (0.1 km² cross-section and 7 m deep), Darss Sill south of the Danish Strait (0.8 km² cross-section and 18 m deep). The Baltic circulation process is controlled by the discharge of freshwater from rivers and from precipitation. This causes an increase in water level in the Baltic with respect to the Kattegat. The difference in water level forces the brackish surface water to flow out of the Baltic Sea. This brackish water will be mixed with more saline marine waters in the Kattegat during its outflow. The outflow will be compensated by the inflow of denser and saline bottom water from the Skagerrak and the Kattegat to fill the deep basins. **Fig. 4.14** shows the processes and the forces that affect the exchange and mixing of the Baltic Sea waters, and **Fig. 4.15** shows a description of a simplified long-term mean circulation scenario.

The large scale circulation of the Baltic Sea is due to a non-linear interaction between the estuarine circulation and exchange with the North Sea waters.

1. This value is based upon the shoreline data available for the marine landscape map in BALANCE delineated by the western HELCOM boundary. The difference between this value and the total Baltic Sea area may be caused by differences in delineation of the sea area or the resolution of shoreline available.

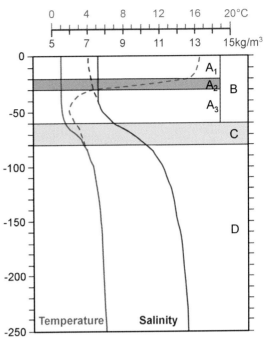

Fig. 4.13. Thermocline stratification in the central Baltic; solid line for winter and dashed line for summer. During the winter season the permanent halocline (C) separates the low salinity cold water (B) from the more saline warmer water deeper in the water column (D). The depth of the halocline increases from 40 m in the Arkona Basin to 60-80 m east of Gotland. During summer, a seasonal thermocline develops at 25-30 m depth (A2) separating the warm upper layer (A1) from a colder intermediate layer (A3). The permanent halocline in the Baltic Proper leads to low bottom water oxygen content. This deep layer is ventilated mainly by lateral advection of North Sea water (by kind permission of Springer Science+Business Media: BACC Author Team 2008: 380, fig. (A.2)).

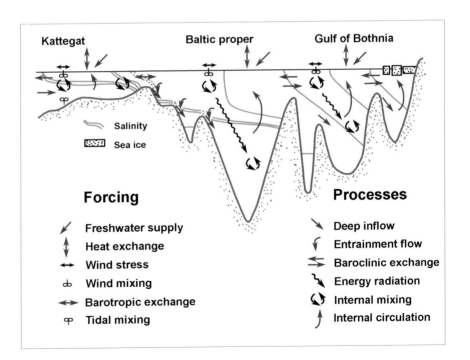

Fig. 4.14. The forces responsible for the exchange and mixing and the process that distribute the water properties in the Baltic (Winsor et al. 2001).

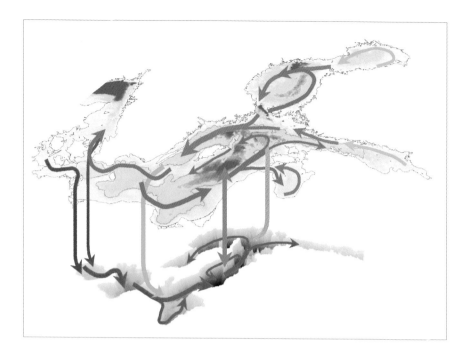

Fig. 4.15. The inflow and the outflow scenario in the Baltic. Green and red arrows are surface and bottom circulation, light green and beige arrows show entrainment and gray arrow indicates diffusion (courtesy of J. Elken. Elken & Matthäus 2008).

Since 1880 there have been 113 major inflows into the Baltic Sea (with no data during World Wars I and II). All inflows have occurred between the end of August and the end of April (**Fig. 4.16**) (BACC Author Team 2008). The seasonal frequency distribution of the major inflows shows that these events are most likely to occur between October and February. They occur in clusters of several years but isolated events also exist. From the beginning of the last century until the mid-1970s, an almost regular pattern was observed in the inflows occurrence. After that the intensity and frequency of these inflows has changed; only a few major events have taken place since then. Only major inflows of large volume (100-250 km³), high salinity (17-25 psu), and oxygen-rich waters can penetrate deep into the Baltic basins renewing their bottom waters and make a significant change in their properties.

The effect of the North Atlantic Oscillation (NAO) on Baltic oceanography

Research on the effect of climatic factors on the Baltic oceanographic and ecological changes has been going on for some decades. As salinity in the Baltic Sea plays an important role in controlling the fauna and flora com-

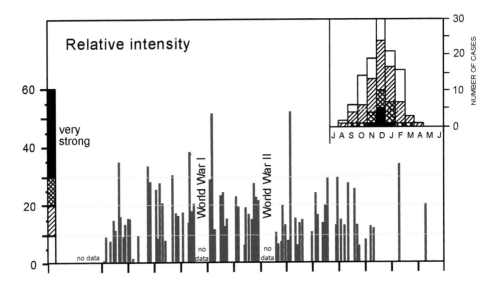

Fig. 4.16. Major Baltic inflows (1880-2005) and their seasonal distribution (upper right) (Matthäus & Franck 1992).

position as well as for the fishery industry, the study of the saline water inflow and predictions for future events are important both from ecological and economical points of view.

Salinity changes in the Baltic Sea have been attributed to irregular pulses of the North Sea penetrating the Danish Straits. Despite the cluster pattern mentioned before, the pulses are irregular and unpredictable as they were almost absent in the 1980s. The North Atlantic Oscillation (NAO) is the major factor of inter-annual variability of the atmospheric circulation in Northern and Central Europe. The NAO is mostly pronounced in amplitude and areal coverage during winter, which accounts for one-third of the total variance in sea level pressure. The tidal dominated North Sea is also controlled by meteorological and climatic factors which have been recently linked to the NAO (Hänninen et al. 2000). The NAO index is calculated as the difference of normalised pressure between the Azores subtropical high and the Icelandic subpolar low (Eriksson 2009). The NAO index provides a measure of the strength of the mid-latitude westerly circulation over the North Atlantic. The index alternate more or less randomly in high or low phases with periodicity of several years. A positive NAO index is associated with strong westerly wind while a negative index value represents weak winds. The freshwater coming from the run-off area to the Baltic Sea is meteorologically mainly of Atlantic origin. During the positive NAO season in the 1980s, there was a substantial increase in the rainfall over the area extending from Northern Germany to the British Isles to Scandinavia. Simultaneously, the Baltic Sea experienced a lack of

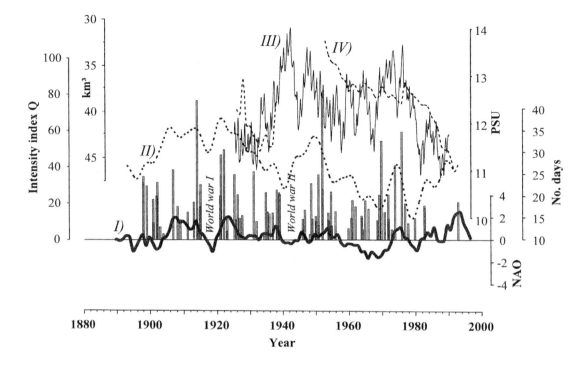

Fig. 4.17. The vertical bars are the major inflow into the Baltic Sea. Line I is the North Atlantic Oscillation index taken at 5 year intervals moving average. Line II is the number of days (decadal filtered values) of the westerly weather type over the British Isles in winter. Line III is the total freshwater runoff (smoothed exponentially) to the Baltic Sea (y-axis inverted). Line IV is the long-term variations of salinity in the deep water (200 m) monitoring station off the island of Gotland (Hänninen et al. 2000).

saline water pulses, which would have increased its salinity. During the years of negative NAO values, from the early 1950s until late 1970s, several pulses penetrated the Danish Straits and salinity remained at a high level in the Baltic Sea (**Fig. 4.17**).

Hanninen et al. (2000) used dynamic regression models to relate the response of the Baltic Sea salinity to hypothetical controlling factors of westerly wind, freshwater runoff, and the NAO. The results of the analysis suggest the existence of a general chain-of-events relationship between the NAO and the subsequent weather effect over the North Sea and the Baltic Sea run-off area. The saline water pulses are more frequent during winter, which is attributed to strong westerly winds over Northern Europe while runoff is reduced considerably due to frozen surface waters in the Baltic catchment area. During positive NAO, winter is mild and the rainfall is above normal in Northern Europe. During a low index the conditions are reversed. Therefore, the appearance of saline water pulses in groups could be explained by higher likelihood of their occurring during a negative NAO period.

Baltic Sea climate

The climate is a result of the complex interaction between the atmospheric, cryospheric (ice cover), hydrospheric (ocean), lithospheric (land), and biospheric (life) enhanced by a non-uniform spatial distribution of incoming solar radiation.

The Baltic Sea climate shows a great deal of variability in different parameters such as ice cover, salinity, runoff, and sea level. The geographic location of the Baltic Sea between the North Atlantic and the Eurasian weather systems leads to large seasonal and inter-annual variation in the low and the high pressure systems. There is a close connection between the large scale atmospheric circulation and the Baltic Sea climate variability. Climate change research is not a straightforward task; many researchers attribute recent changes to anthropogenic sources and the greenhouse effect, while others consider these changes natural caused by volcanic and solar forcing (Omstedt et al. 2004b).

Research has been conducted on the effect of NAO on regional air temperature (Chen & Hellström 1999), monthly circulation climatology (Chen 2000), the relationship between circulation indices and temperature (Jacobeit et al. 2001), ice cover and winter circulation (Omstedt & Chen 2001), and developing a model for sea level variation (Gustafsson & Andersson 2001). A general conclusion from these studies is that there is a close interrelation between atmospheric variation (interpreted by various circulation indices) and parameters from the Baltic Sea region such as temperature, ice cover, and sea level.

In their work, Omstedt and his colleagues (Omstedt et al. 2004b) studied climate change in the Baltic Sea over the last 200 years and found several interesting relationships between different parameters (**Fig. 4.18**). The increase in air temperature and sea level is correlated with the increase in the anti-cyclonic circulation, while the change in the magnitude of the seasonal temperature cycle and ice cover is slightly correlated with the reduced southwesterly wind type.

The study indicates that the Baltic Sea climate change for the past 200 years (averaged over 15 year periods) has become more influenced by anti-cyclonic circulation (clock-wise airflow in the northern hemisphere). The study also shows that the increased frequency of anti-cyclonic circulation and increased westerly winds have resulted in a slightly warmer climate with a reduced seasonal temperature cycle and reduced ice cover. The increase in sea level variation in the Baltic Sea can be partially attributed to global sea level rise and to changes in circulation.

Omstedt and his colleagues conclude (Omstedt et al. 2004b): there is a positive trend in air temperature, sea level, and frequency of anti-cyclonic circulation and westerly wind types; the major climatic changes occurred at the end of the 19th century which could be related to end of the Little

Fig. 4.18. Anomalies for the climate records together with the circulation types that describes the rotation of the atmospheric circulation. Red indicates anti-cyclonic and blue cyclonic circulation. (a) Air temperatures and anti cyclonic circulation; (b) sea level and anti-cyclonic circulation; (c) seasonal index and cyclonic circulation; and (d) ice cover and cyclonic circulation (Omstedt et al. 2004b).

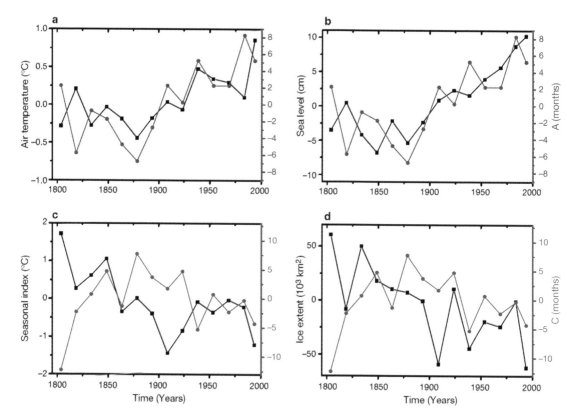

Ice Age; the observed changes in the Baltic Sea climate can be related to atmospheric circulation and natural variability, if one ignores the anthropogenic intervention. The question still to be answered by more research is how anthropogenic activities affect the large scale atmospheric circulation and how these two can influence the Baltic Sea region.

5. Wood as material

Charlotte Gjelstrup Björdal

Wood has been one of the most important construction and building materials throughout human history. It is readily available, simple to form and provides a very strong material for advanced constructions. There exist a huge number of wood species which vary widely in their physical and chemical properties (Wood_handbook 2010). This natural variation has been known, explored, and used throughout history. For boatbuilding the selection of wood species is important in order to meet different requirements for strength, flexibility, elasticity and durability.

5.1 Structure and classification

Trees are divided into two main groups: softwoods (gymnosperms) and hardwoods (angiosperms). Pine (*Pinus sylvestris*), spruce (*Picea abies*) and larch (*Larix*) are examples of softwood, whereas oak (*Quercus sp*), elm (*Ulmus*) and beech (*Fagus*) are typical hardwoods.

The two types of trees are different and have a different structure in regards to growing in their natural habitat and and of the wood material itself (**Fig. 5.1**).

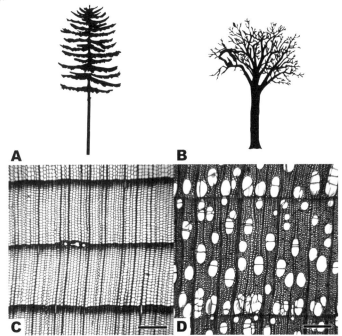

Fig. 5.1. Schematics of softwood (left) and hardwood (right) structures. They have different silhouettes when growing (A, B), and the wood tissue also differs. Softwood (C) has a more simple structure than hardwood (D) (courtesy of R. Rowell).

The growth of a tree is controlled by the cambium, which is a very thin layer situated just beneath the bark. Here new wood cells are formed and transferred into different mature wood elements. The outer part of a tree's stem (trunk) is called the sapwood. This is the "living" part of the wood where water transport takes place. As the tree grows, the sapwood continuously dies and is transformed into heartwood (**Fig. 5.2**). This leads to formation of more extractives and water transport ceases (Haygreen & Bowyer 1989). In some wood species, heartwood can be identified by its darker colour (**Fig. 5.3**). The heartwood of many wood species is more biologically durable than sapwood.

In temperate climates, annual rings are formed inside a trunk, often with two types of cells, depending on the season. Early-wood cells, often thin walled, are formed during the first part of the growing season, whereas late-wood cells, often thick-walled and therefore more dense, are formed during the second part of the growing season (Rowell 2005). The variation in density creates the well-known annual ring patterns, which can be identified with the naked eye (**Fig. 5.3**). The width of annual rings is closely correlated with the local climate and growing conditions – a fact that provides the basis for dendrochronology.

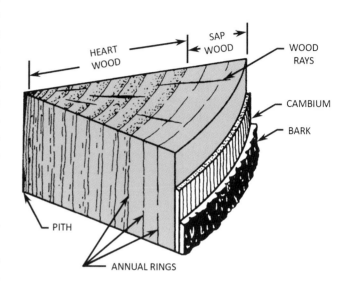

Fig. 5.2. Pie cut of a generalised piece of wood showing different elements in its structure. In the thin cambium layer just beneath the bark, new wood cells are continuously produced. Sapwood is the outer living part of the tree (courtesy of R. Rowell).

Fig. 5.3. A disc of a young pine showing annual rings of different widths. The light appearance of the sapwood is easily distinguished from the dark zone of heartwood (photo: C. Gjelstrup Björdal).

5.2 Wood anatomy

Softwoods and hardwoods have clearly different anatomical structures, but to distinguish between the different groups of hardwood and softwood species demands skill, as many wood species have anatomic features that sometimes might be seemingly identical to an untrained eye. Softwoods have the simplest anatomy with only a few cell types. Here tracheids, ray tracheids and parenchyma cells constitute the major cell types, whereas hardwoods have a broader variety of cell types, such as fibre tracheids, libriform fibres, vessel elements and parenchyma cells (Panshin & Zeeuw 1980). The observation of wood is always carried out in three well defined directions: transverse section, radial section and tangential section. The anatomy of different types of fibres in longitudinal and transversal orientations gives a unique pattern/fingerprint which is used for identification of the actual wood species.

In softwoods, 90-95% of the volume is occupied by fibres called tracheids, making the structure of softwoods quite homogeneous (**Fig. 5.4**).

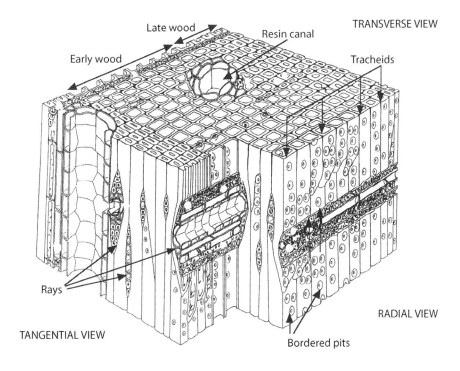

Fig. 5.4. Simplified anatomical features of a softwood species, viewed in 3-D plane. A cut in transverse section shows the tracheids as longitudinal individual "straws" with large openings in the centre for water conduction. Early-wood tracheids have larger openings than late-wood cells. Small pits ensure connection to adjacent cells. Rays are important horizontal structures that are best viewed in radial and tangential plane. Resin canals are present as large openings (drawing: C. Gjelstrup Björdal, modified and redrawn after Howard & Manwiller 1969).

These are, put simply, straws with an empty central channel (lumen) dedicated for the transportation of water, nutrients and extractives. The tracheids are aligned in the longitudinal direction oriented parallel to the stem axis. The length and diameter of the tracheids can be up to 7 mm long and 25-45 µm wide, respectively. They are "glued" together into a wood matrix by the middle lamella.

The structure of hardwood tissue is in principle similar, but the large variety of cell types, including vessels, gives a visually more heterogeneous structure. A cross-section of a hardwood (oak) and a softwood (pine), observed by light microscopy, is shown in **Fig. 5.5** for comparison.

A close-up of the cell wall structure is simplified in **Fig. 5.6**, showing lumen (empty space in the centre of each cell), the primary cell wall, the secondary cell wall, and the compound middle lamellae (Eaton & Hale 1993). The secondary cell wall is divided into three layers and the different orientation of the micro-fibrils in the layers is indicated. The cell wall in early-wood is thin (ca. 2 µm), whereas in late-wood it is much thicker (ca. 4.3 µm).

5.3 Wood chemistry and physics

Wood is principally composed of carbon, hydrogen and oxygen which constitute the wood polymers: cellulose, hemicelluloses and lignin. Between 40-50% of the total cell wall mass is cellulose, 25-40% hemicelluloses, and 18-33% lignin. Cellulose is a polymer of 8,000-10,000 units of glucose, whereas hemicelluloses are shorter polymers of other sugars. The long cellulose chains are organised into larger units, called micro-fibrils,

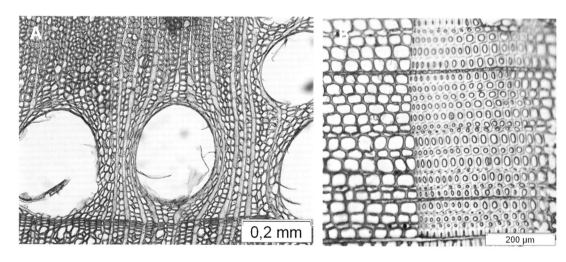

0,2 mm

200 µm

Fig. 5.5. Cross-sections of oak (A) (Quercus robur) *and pine (B)* (Pinus sylvestris) *show the different micro-structure of soft- and hardwoods. One of the most significant differences is the vessels (large circular openings) of hardwoods (photos: C. Gjelstrup Björdal).*

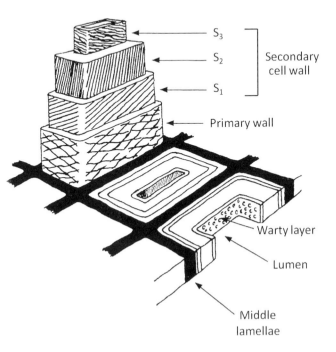

Fig. 5.6. A transverse section of three softwood tracheids illustrating the cell wall structure on a microscopic level. Lumen is in the centre of each tracheid, and the cell wall consists of a primary wall and a secondary wall. The latter is divided into three layers (modified and re-drawn after Eaton & Hale 1993).

and embedded in hemicelluloses and lignin (Hedges 1990). These are known to provide the wood with its excellent strength properties, and are orientated in different angles in the secondary cell walls layers. Lignin is considered as the "glue" between fibres, both on a micro-, ultra- and nano-level and is a complex three-dimensional polymer composed mainly of phenylpropane units. Softwoods and hardwoods differ in types of lignin that influence the natural durability of the wood.

The distribution of cellulose, hemicelluloses and lignin varies within the cell wall layers. The highest concentration of lignin is found in the middle lamella area and the highest concentration of cellulose is found in the S_2 layer. These distributions do influence the sensitivity towards biological degradation on a cell wall level (Rowell 2005).

5.4 Durability of wood species

The natural durability of wood species varies. The resistance toward wood-degrading micro-organisms is generally closely related to amount and type of lignin as well as extractives and silica content. In heartwood the amount of extractives are generally higher than in sapwood. This makes heartwood the most durable part of most timbers. Durability of a certain wood exposed in nature depends on the interaction between the specific wood species and the surrounding environment (Eaton & Hale 1993). It has been observed that durability of one wood species differs in ground contact, above ground contact, in a water column and within marine sediments. For example, the durability of oak and pine heartwood is almost similar when exposed in soil and ground contact under rapid degradation, but in aquatic environments, with an absence of marine borers, oak heartwood is found to be much more durable than pine sap- and heartwood. As one can expect, oak has been the most attractive timber for shipbuilding in Northern European countries throughout the centuries.

6. Wood degraders in the Baltic Sea

Christin Appelqvist

6.1 Marine wood borers

Marine crustaceans and bivalves effectively fragment submerged wood. In this way they have an ecologically important effect in the turn-over of organic material in the sea, especially in mangrove systems, but also in other places.

The wood-boring bivalves belong to the suborder *Pholadina*, which contains the two related families, *Teredinidae* and *Pholadidae*. The Teredinids, usually called shipworms, are obligate wood borers, except for the mud-boring genera *Kuphus* and seagrass-dwelling *Zachsia*. There are in total 66 species within this family, and six of those reproduce in Northern Europe (Turner 1966). The one causing most economic problems is the cosmopolite *Teredo navalis*, which is the only species found active today in the southeastern part of the Baltic Sea. Of the wood-boring Pholadids, *Martesiianae* and *Xylophagainae*, it is only members of the latter subfamily that ingest wood. The largest morphological difference between shipworms and other bivalves is the reduced shells that function primarily as a drilling tool rather than for protection. In *Teredinidae* the nearly hemispherical shells cover only the anterior part of the animal, and a thin calcareous layer deposited on the walls of their burrows protects the rest of the worm-like body. Species in this family have also two associated calcified structures at the posterior end, called pallets. Pallets and calcified tube walls are absent in *Xylophagainae*. After settlement, shipworms bore into the wood and seldom along the wood's surface. The wood looks almost intact except for the small entrance holes. The damage is therefore hard to detect by the eye, especially under water. The devastation is often discovered late in the degrading process when the burrows are exposed.

In contrast to shipworms that penetrate wood, wood-boring crustaceans (gribbles) mainly gnaw and burrow at the surface. In areas with very little tidal movements, such as Skagerrak and Kattegat, wood attacked by gribbles often appears hourglass shaped because the predominant attacks occur close to mean sea level. The most common species are members of the genera *Limnoria*, *Sphaeroma* and *Chelura*. Together they degrade wood from the intertidal zone to depths of 1,000 m, and are widely distributed from sub-polar to tropical latitudes. They show low fecundity, extended parental care, and migrate to new substrata as juveniles and

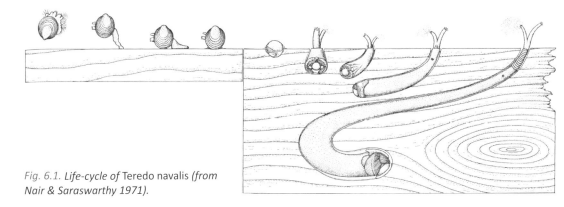

Fig. 6.1. Life-cycle of Teredo navalis (from
Nair & Saraswarthy 1971).

young adults. At present it is unclear whether wood-boring crustaceans
host cellulolytic bacteria; however, it is known that cellulose is degraded
during gut passage of Limnoriids. Members of the family *Sphaeromatidae*,
which don't ingest wood, break down the wood mechanically and in this
way also cause extensive damage.

6.2 The biology and life cycle of *Teredo navalis*

Infestation of wood by shipworms
occurs during the larval phase of
their life cycle (**Fig. 6.1**). The larvae of *T. navalis* are planktotroph-
ic, meaning they have to feed on
plankton during the free-swimming larval phase (**Fig. 6.2**). After
about 14 days in the water column
at a size of approximately 0.25 mm
they are mature enough to settle
on to wood. If no suitable substrate
is available they can survive for an
additional two weeks. After suc-

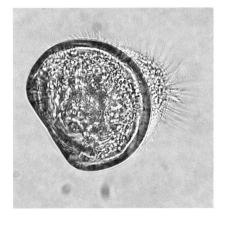

Fig. 6.2. Four-day-
old larvae of Teredo
navalis (74 x 80 µm)
(photo: C. Appelqvist,

cessful settlement they pass through the critical metamorphosis stage.
The larva then changes from a juvenile to an adult that will never naturally
leave the piece of wood. As the adults grow they follow the grain of wood,
avoid knots or joints and seldom interfere with others or break into the
burrow of their neighbours. Depending on age, population density, kind
of wood and the environmental factors, the adult size of *T. navalis* ranges
from a few millimetres up to one metre. As they grow at the anterior end
they secrete a calcareous layer on the walls of the burrow. It is only at
the posterior end close to the siphons that the animal is attached to this
calcified tube. The boring is performed through repeated rasping move-

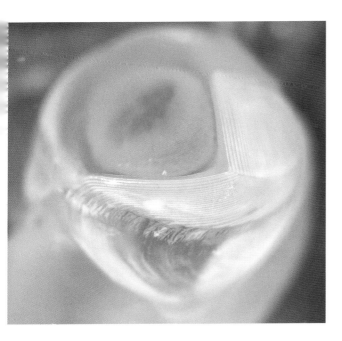

Fig. 6.3. Shell and muscular foot (ø 5 mm) of an adult Teredo navalis *(photo: C. Appelqvist).*

Fig. 6.4. A pair of pallets of Teredo navalis *(5x2 mm) (photo: C. Appelqvist).*

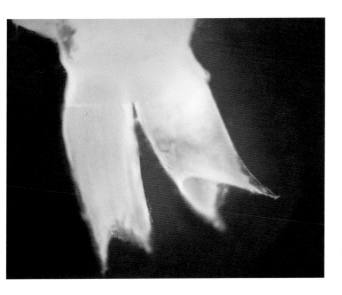

ments by the fine serrated shells (**Fig. 6.3**), which make a perfectly circular burrow within the wood. Subsequently small wood particles are transported by ciliated movement to the mouth and become ingested. The shipworm can assimilate carbohydrates from the wood with help from unique endosymbiotic bacteria (*Teredinibacter turnerae*) that produce cellulolytic enzymes (Distel et al. 2002). The symbionts are hosted intracellularly in the gills of the shipworm. They are never in direct contact with wood or with the digestive system, so the cellulolytic enzymes must be transported to the digestive system in some way. However, this mechanism is yet unknown and more research is needed. At the posterior end of the animal is a pair of retractable siphons and the two species-specific pallets (**Fig. 6.4**). By sealing their burrow with the pallets they can avoid unfavourable conditions in the surrounding water, and survive for at least three weeks upon stored glycogen. The tube-like siphons (**Fig. 6.5**) are used for filtration of plankton and obtaining an oxygen supply. By filter feeding they receive nutritional lipids and proteins (Mann & Gallager 1985a). However, this mussel can survive and reproduce without plankton feeding for at least two years since the symbionts are also capable of fixing nitrogen. Thereby they provide an internal source of nitrogen to supplement the host's protein-deficient diet. *T. navalis* has a relatively short generation time and becomes sexually mature at an age of three weeks at temperatures of 20°C (Culliney 1975). This is probably an adaptation to living in an ephemeral habitat. In temperate waters this spe-

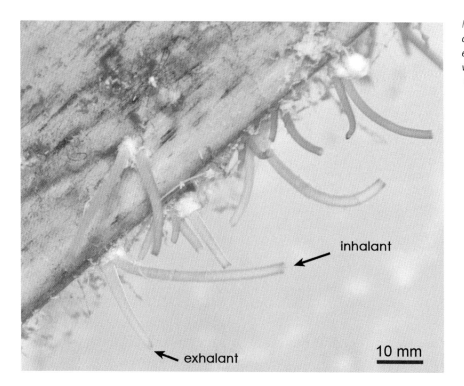

Fig. 6.5. *Siphons of* Teredo navalis *extended from wood (photo: C. Appelqvist).*

cies spawns at temperatures above 11-12°C. Male gamets are extruded into the water and then taken into the mantel cavity of female individuals through the inhalant siphon. After internal fertilisation the larvae develop in a brood pouch for two weeks before they are dispersed.

6.3 The ecology of *Teredo navalis*

Several environmental factors of seawater affect the physiological and ecological behaviour of shipworms. However, the physical key parameters are salinity, temperature, dissolved oxygen, ocean currents and the availability of wooden substrate (Turner 1966). The occurrence, abundance and intensity of shipworm attacks are dependent on these factors, which usually vary widely from year to year. These climate fluctuations contribute to the periodically reoccurring devastations often separated by long periods of no attacks in an area. The distribution pattern of a shipworm species correlated to environmental key factors might also vary between geographically-distinguished localities due to genetic variation and local adaptations. For example, the worldwide-distributed species *T. navalis* shows a wide range of tolerance for different environmental parameters.

Already in the beginning of the 18th century scientists believed that salinity limited the distribution of Teredinids. Later on this hypothesis was supported by many studies but also rejected by recent investigations. Studies have shown that adults of estuarine shipworm species survive and develop larvae in aquaria at salinity conditions outside the salinity range in nature. This is also confirmed by experiments on larvae that showed a wider salinity tolerance in the lab than in the ocean. These studies suggest that salinity alone is not the determining factor for the distribution of shipworms. The responses to salinity of *T. navalis* show a remarkable similarity throughout different parts of the world. Local adaptations might have evolved in such a way that each population should preferably be studied individually, especially in estuarine regions. Normal boring activities by adults generally occur in salinities down to 7-9 psu, with salinity less than 4-6 psu being lethal, with the exception of the Black Sea where 8 psu seems to be lethal. Reproduction is possible in salinities above 8-10 psu (Sordyl et al. 1998; HELCOM data base). There is an assumption that bivalve larvae are less tolerant than adults of extremes in salinity; however, this is not likely the case. Experiments have shown that the upper salinity tolerance of larvae of *T. navalis* was far less than that of adults, but the lower limit was similar. The adults remain active between 7-45 psu and the larvae were active at 6-31 psu (Hoagland 1986). In this study the lethal limit was fixed to 5 psu for larvae of *T. navalis*. Notably the age of bivalve larvae is crucial for the resistance to salinity variations, and more experiments are needed.

Temperature is an important factor influencing not only the biological systems but also hydrographical conditions, for example, it influences precipitation thereby affecting salinity. For shipworms temperature is a limiting factor for reproduction, growth and geographical distribution. One explanation for the range extension of *T. navalis* in the southern Baltic has been that the species can tolerate lower salinity due to increased temperature. However, this hypothesis has not been tested. In fact, for many invertebrates and vertebrates, an increased environmental temperature results in an increased energy metabolism but also increased basal metabolic rate. This may in turn lead to less energy available for osmoregulation and thus makes them less tolerant to extreme salinities. *T. navalis* is known from localities all over the world and the species can withstand a wide range of temperatures. In cold water, such as in Sweden, Germany, and in the Black Sea, adults can tolerate temperatures that range from -1.4°C to 30°C and are most active between 15-25°C (Roch 1932). For shipworms in temperate oceans, spawning activity is stimulated by rising temperatures in spring. In the Atlantic, *T. navalis* has a long spawning season starting in early summer and lasting to late fall. The species spawns at temperatures above 11-15°C (Culliney 1975; Loosanoff & Davis 1963). Larvae are more sensitive to lower temperatures than adults. Laboratory observations have found active larvae at 10-29°C, and temperatures below 7.5°C or above 30°C were lethal (Hoagland 1986; M´Gonigle 1926).

Many well-preserved wrecks in the Baltic Sea are situated in oxygen-depleted areas. In these environments the deterioration process by both microorganisms and invertebrates is very slow. Therefore, oxygen is an important parameter to be included in consideration of attacks by shipworms, yet there is a lack of experiments on their requirements for dissolved oxygen. The available data today are principally about oxygen consumption in different stress situations, but adults of T. navalis have been observed active when the oxygen level fell to 0.98 mg O_2/l (Roch 1932).

Fig. 6.6. X-ray image of a wooden panel submerged for six months off the Swedish west coast, showing hundreds of shipworms inside (photo: C. Appelqvist).

6.4 The effect of *Teredo* attacks on shipwrecks

Shipworms perform a vital ecosystem function by degrading terrestrial material in the sea, yet they simultaneously cause extensive damage to economically and culturally important marine wooden structures. Unlike other marine biofouling, damage caused by shipworms is an irreversible process – the consumed wood is gone forever. However, on-going degradation can be stopped, for example, by moving an active vessel into fresh water (below 4 psu), drain an active ship's hull of bilge or ballast water for at least one month, or cover a shipwreck with *in-situ* protection methods. The infestation takes place when a piece of wood is submerged or when a wooden wreck is exposed during the larval season. The occurrence and extent of attacks depends upon, among other factors, larval supply, competition with other fouling organisms, the success of metamorphosis, and the species of wood. The growth rate of shipworms varies greatly between geographical locations and is also directly related to the prevailing hydrographical conditions of the surrounding water. However, a supplement of nutritionally-rich food in the form of phytoplankton seems to have no effect on the growth rate, at least when they have enough wood on which to feed (Mann & Gallager 1985a). Instead, growth is highly dependent on the number of individuals that have settled in the same piece of wood and compete for space (Norman 1977). The rate of growth varies also with age and where they are in the reproductive cycle. Studies in the western Atlantic on T. navalis show maximum growth lengths of 32 mm in the first month, and up to 400 mm in one year at 20-23°C (Mann & Gallager 1985b). In Scandinavian waters the highest growth rates occur at temperatures over 15°C and the longest specimen found after 18 months measured 270 mm, and 590 mm after 36 months (Norman 1977; Steenstrup Kristensen 1979). Growth was absent at temperatures below 5°C. Adult shipworms have few predators and the life span of T. navalis can be at least 3 years. With a growth rate of 0.5-1 mm per day in temperate waters like those in Scandinavia, a 20 cm-long piece of wood will be completely consumed by T. navalis within a year (**Fig. 6.6**).

Fig. 6.7. The fishing vessel Rio heavily infested by shipworms and other marine organisms after six years on the seabed (photo: Staffan von Arbin, Bohusläns Museum).

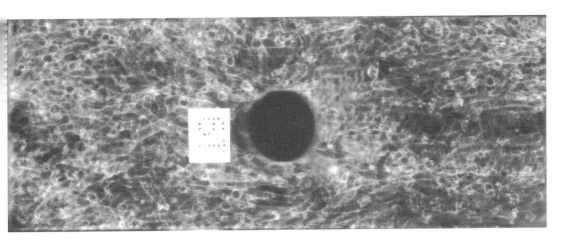

A study on the degradation rate of a wooden wreck was conducted between 2003-2009 along the Swedish west coast. A 15 m-long oak-built fishing vessel was submerged at a depth of 16 m. Within a few years, the hull was totally infested by shipworms and after six years it was completely destroyed. In 2011, the main part of the hull is still standing erect on the seabed but is starting to fall apart. Many of the shipworms are dead but the calcified tubes from old boreholes and the relatively intact surface layer of the wood is still holding the structure together (**Fig. 6.7**).

6.5 Detection of shipworm attacks

The entrance hole where the larvae first settle on to the wood's surface will remain small and enlarge only slightly during the life span of a ship-worm. Therefore, it is hard to detect shipworm attacks: the internal damage caused by these animals could be enormous with relatively little trace on the surface. Normally the siphons are extended out of the entrance holes but will quickly be retracted if they get disturbed. An additional challenge when looking for signs of shipworm is to find the siphons or the small entrance holes among all the other biofouling organisms. Hard substrata are colonised rapidly in the ocean due to the extreme competition for space among species. Many sessile marine organisms are filter-feeders that consume plankton such as shipworm larvae. Consequently the structure of a biofouling community will affect the risk of shipworm attack. However, even a well-developed biofouling community in a piece of wood does not necessarily work as protection for infestation by ship-worms. Dominant biofouling taxa include other bivalves, bryozoans, anemones, hydroids, polychaetes, barnacles, seastars, porifera, tunicates, and algae.

The simplest way to detect if wood is attacked by shipworms is to remove all the biofouling and then search for entrance holes on the surface. If living specimens are present, they will extend their siphons after a few minutes. Despite extensive internal damage a shipwreck that has been attacked by shipworm of the family *Teredinidae* may remain intact for a long time after infestation because the burrows of these shipworms are lined with calcium. This supporting structure helps to hold the piece of wood together, although the material strength is severely reduced. Such infested wood is very fragile and may easily break upon impact with other objects. In marine environments where small wood-eating crustaceans are found in the same habitat, the calcified tubes of the shipworms can be exposed and the infestation is more easily discovered (**Fig. 6.8**).

Fig. 6.8. Calcareous tubes made by Teredo navalis *(photo: J. Havenhand).*

6.6 Fungal and bacterial decay
Charlotte Gjelstrup Björdal

Biodegradation of wood is an important process for the recycling of carbon in nature, where the wood polymers (lignin, cellulose and hemicelluloses) are decomposed by micro-organisms, liberating carbon dioxide, water and mineral elements. Decomposition of wood in aquatic ecosystems involves a large number of different specialised organisms such as molluscs, crustaceans, fungi, and bacteria (Eaton 1993).

The activity of molluscs and crustaceans is, as discussed, restricted to waters of certain salinity, temperature, and oxygen concentrations, whereas wood-degrading fungi and bacteria are present in all types of environments such as estuaries, lakes, rivers, and in the sea and oceans world-wide. In brackish and freshwater ecosystems, where marine borers are absent, the biological decay of wood is solely controlled by specialised wood-degrading fungi and bacteria.

Fig. 6.9. Fractured part of oak (Quercus robur) timber from a submerged 17th-century wreck found in the Baltic Sea. The outer-most degraded surface layer has turned black by soft-rot fungi attack in combination with encrustations of mineral and oak tannins. Erosion bacteria decay beneath the surface does not affect the color of the wood. In this example the majority of the wood's interior is still sound (photo: C. Gjelstrup Björdal).

The understanding of the role of wood-degrading fungi in aquatic environments was gained in the 1940s (Mouzouras 1989; Hyde & Pointing 2000), but it was not until the 1980s that the importance of bacterial degradation was verified (Björdal et al. 1999). Today, more than 500 different fungal species have been found to degrade wood, whereas the identity and variety of bacterial species is still unknown.

Compared to decay by mollusc and crustaceans, fungal and bacteria decay takes place at a much slower rate. Shipworms can decompose wood timbers within years, whereas the microbial degradation takes decades, centuries, or millennia depending on the environment and actual wood species. Both fungi and bacteria are very small organisms not visible to the naked eye, and the decay takes place at a fibre level where carbohydrates are extracted from the sound cell wall (Blanchette et al. 1990). This process starts at the wood surface and proceeds slowly inwards, resulting in a soft and fragile decomposed wood material. In **Fig. 6.9**, a wet oak timber submerged in the Baltic Sea for 300 years is fractured: the surface is degraded by fungi and bacteria and the wood has become dark in colour. The microbial decay weakens the wood, which makes it more sensitive to direct physical damage and environmental forces.

6.6.1 Aquatic wood-degrading fungi

Fungi in aquatic environments that are able to degrade wood material are true wood degraders. It has been found that they mainly belong to the group of *Ascomycetes* and *Fungi imperfecti* and cause soft-rot decay of the wood. They degrade cellulose, hemicellulose, and lignin, although there is preferential decay of cellulose and hemicelluloses (Eaton & Hale 1993). Soft-rot fungi use enzymatic tools for their degradation and it is concluded that soft-rot fungi have enzymes for degradation of cellulose and hemicelluloses, whereas enzymes for lignin degradation are less active or not fully developed. The processes are still poorly understood (Pointing & Hyde 2000). The intensity of decay varies and is dependent on the fungal species in question, the environment and the wood species.

Some examples of common soft-rot degraders are *Cirrenalia macrocephala*, *Lulworthia* sp., *Zalerion maritimum*, *Ceriosporopsis Halima*, and *Humicola alopallonella*. They are found in most waters world-wide, although there seems to be a large variation in their frequency, which might be related to the different environmental variation in salinity, temperature, and other factors (Kohlmeyer & Kohlmeyer 1979). In the Baltic Sea several different species have been found, and *Phialophora fastigata* is one of the species that is present in the whole Baltic Sea, including the west coast of Sweden (Henningsson 1976).

Growth and reproduction

Aquatic fungi are fascinating organisms with filamentous growth. They produce long, thin threads (most ranging from 2 to 10 μm in diameter) called hyphae. These grow continuously, forming mycelia which expand into large invisible networks that are able to degrade large timber constructions. They colonise the wood material by penetrating the anatomical openings of the wood. In the phase of reproduction they release high numbers of motile spores, which are spread into the water and transported to new areas where some, by chance, will attach to wooden surfaces and start to develop new hyphae and initiate decay. Marine fungi have spores that are specially "designed" for a successful dispersal and colonisation in turbulent oceans, seas, rivers and running waters. The morphology of the ascospores and conidia are fascinating as they have unusual "arms" and appendages that easily stick to the wood surface (Eaton & Hale 1993).

Soft-rot decay pattern in wood

The decay by aquatic soft-rot fungi is divided into two types, where Type 1 is very common and Type 2 is rare (Mouzouras 1989). Type 1, which is described here, is characterised by hyphal infestation of wood through its

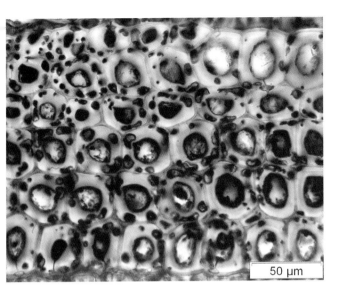

rays and pits, in order to get to the cell lumen. From here, the hyphae penetrate the cellulose-rich secondary cell wall, where degradation continues. Hyphae move into adjacent fibres by penetration of the cell wall, and in a short amount of time a small area of the wood tissue is infected. The typical pattern of soft rot can be detected and observed by light microscopy (**Fig. 6.10**). In cross-section the fungal attack is seen as holes of variable sizes within the cell wall and soft-rot cavities, following the microfibrils of the secondary cell wall, seen in longitudinal sections. Decay of the wood and the cell wall proceeds until the entire secondary cell wall is decomposed.

Fig. 6.10. Typical soft-rot decay viewed in a transverse section of softwood and examined by light microscopy: varying sizes of holes produced by fungal growth in the secondary cell wall (photo: C. Gjelstrup Björdal).

Environmental factors affecting the decay rate caused by soft-rot fungi

Several factors have an impact on the decay rate caused by soft-rot fungi. Temperature, salinity, oxygen, nutrients, and pH are the most important factors and each species have their specific limits and optima. There are also complicated interactions between the parameters such as salinity and temperature, nitrogen source and temperature. The understanding of these processes is still embryonic. Most data on the requirement for growth are based on experiments and carried out in laboratories. Most are based on studies on agar plates, and only a few are carried out in liquid media. The access to oxygen is different in these experiments and it is most likely that the results obtained do not fully reflect the true situation in nature.

6.6.2 Aquatic wood-degrading bacteria

Bacteria are single-celled organisms, called prokaryotes, and morphologically "primitive" compared to fungi (eukaryotes). Their role is, however, crucial for the turnover of organic and inorganic material in nature, and it has been found that bacteria are the predominant degraders of lignocelluloses in aquatic ecosystems. Studies on diversity of bacteria in aquatic environments show that communities in oceans, freshwater bodies and estuaries are very similar. Estuaries have the largest diversity, in terms of clone numbers, probably as a result of the mixing of bacteria communities from river, oceans and estuaries (Crump et al. 1999).

Wood-degrading bacteria belong to the group of heterotrophic bacteria, which are bacteria that extract energy from high and low molecular organic compounds. Two types of bacteria are found to degrade wood in aquatic environments: tunnelling bacteria and erosion bacteria. Both are named after their specific characteristics of attack. Both types of bacteria are rod-shaped and move by gliding. They are found to degrade wood in marine and freshwater environments world-wide, and are regarded as cosmopolitan organisms. Despite extensive efforts to isolate and cultivate them during recent decades, their true identity is still unknown. As a consequence, almost nothing is known about their tools for degradation or environmental requirements.

Description of erosion bacteria and tunnelling bacteria

Tunnelling bacteria have an unique ability to degrade preservative-treated wood and naturally durable timbers in contact with soils, which has made this group of bacteria the special focus of the wood industry (Eaton & Hale 1993). The bacteria are able to degrade all wood polymers, which include lignin and lignin-rich areas such as the compound middle lamellae, and are therefore regarded as the ultimate degraders. Tunnelling bacteria are also active in aquatic environments where they are often found degrading the wood surface layer together with soft-rot fungi.

Erosion bacteria have been of significant interest to conservators and archaeologists as they are the main degraders of waterlogged archaeological wood. They have the ability to degrade cellulose and hemicelluloses, but not the lignin-rich part of the wood cell wall, the compound middle lamellae. This inability is verified by chemical and morphological studies. Another characteristic is their ability to degrade wood under near-anaerobic conditions, which includes timbers situated in sediment under the seabed, as well as interior parts of thicker wooden construction with oxygen depletion. Recent research on their identity using modern DNA techniques show that they most likely belong to the group of *Cytophaga-Flavobacteria* cluster, which is a large group present in both terrestrial and aquatic environments (Landy et al. 2008).

Both types of bacteria start the decay of wood by an initial attachment to the wood surface. From here they enter the wood structure, reproduce, and spread.

Bacterial decay pattern

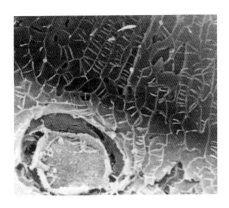

Fig. 6.11. Tunneling bacteria attack on wood cell wall observed by scanning electron microscopy: tunnels with typical perpendicular cross walls are formed (photo: C. Gjelstrup Björdal).

Tunnelling bacteria form individual tunnels within the wood's cell wall. Each bacterium is located in the front-end of the tunnel, and form characteristic "wall" deposits during decay (**Fig. 6.11**). This divides each tunnel into many sections. As they reproduce by dividing, new tunnels develop. This activity results in a heterogeneous branching pattern of tunnels. In aquatic environments both soft-rot and tunnelling bacterial activity are restricted to the outer-most millimetres of submerged timbers, as both types of degraders require a relatively high oxygen concentration for decay and will not advance into the more anoxic atmosphere inside the wood.

Erosion bacteria are named due to their way of eroding the wood cell walls (**Fig. 6.12**). They are gram-negative rod-shaped organisms with varying sizes: 1-8 µm long and 0.5-0.9 µm in diameter (Björdal et al. 2000). Invasion starts through rays and pits, from where bacteria enter the cell lumen. Here, single bacteria attach to the cell wall and locally penetrate the S3 cell wall layer in order to access to the cellulose-rich S2 layer. The lignin-rich

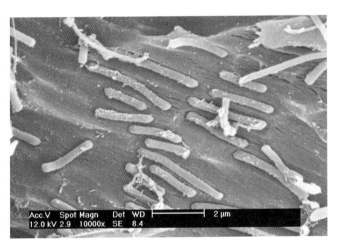

Acc.V Spot Magn   Det WD   2 µm
12.0 kV 2.9 10000x SE 8.4

Fig. 6.12. Scanning electron micrograph showing rod-shaped erosion bacteria aligned in individual troughs following the micro fibrillar orientation of the secondary cell wall layer. These bacteria are able to degrade timber both in the water column and in sediment (photo: C. Gjelstrup Björdal).

middle lamellae remains seemingly unaffected, even at very advanced stages of decay, which is one of the main characteristics of this type of decay (**Fig. 6.13**) (Daniel & Nilsson 1986; Kim & Singh 2000).

After decay, the bacteria leave behind a slimy, granular residual material that remains in the fibre. In moderately degraded wood, a characteristic decay pattern occurs where apparently sound tracheids, adjacent to heavily degraded ones, form a chessboard-like pattern (**Fig. 6.14**). Decay

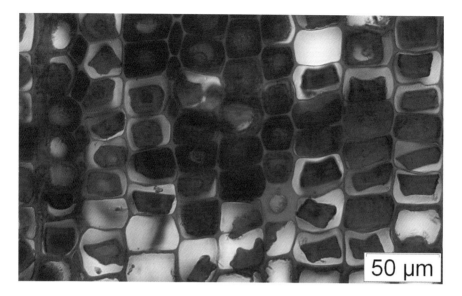

Fig. 6.13. Transversal section of pine (Pinus sylvestris) showing a total decay of the wood cell wall by erosion bacteria, leaving behind the middle lamellae as a fragile lignin skeleton. The cell wall material is transformed into a slimy residual material that remains inside some of the fibres as loose material. Transversal section (photo: C. Gjelstrup Björdal).

Fig. 6.14. In moderately degraded areas, erosion bacteria decay give raise to a chess-like pattern composed of degraded (red) respectively sound (white) wood fibres. Tranversal section of Pinus sylvestris (photo: C. Gjelstrup Björdal).

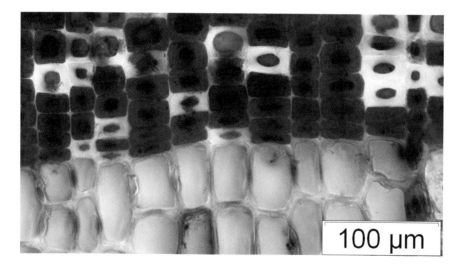

proceeds slowly from the wood exterior and inwards until all cellulose-rich areas in the wood are utilised. This process may go on for thousands of years.

Environmental factors that affect the speed of decay

As neither tunnelling bacteria nor erosion bacteria have yet been cultured and identified, experimental work that could reveal their environmental requirements has been unachievable. Knowledge so far is based mainly on field studies. As both tunnelling bacteria and erosion bacteria seem to be present in all types of aquatic environments world-wide, they are probably very tolerant organisms if we regard them as a group. Regarding oxygen concentrations, it is generally agreed that low levels do de-activate tunnelling bacteria, but not the erosion bacteria which seem to tolerate near anaerobic conditions. The activity of erosion bacteria is reduced but not stopped by decreased oxygen concentrations, for example, within deeper layers of sediment. Erosion bacteria are found to degrade wood at low temperatures, great depths, at high salinities, and in extreme environments like the deep sea (up to 5,000 m) (Kohlmeyer 1980).

6.6.3 Importance of wood species

Some timbers have a reputation for being very durable when submerged in water, but often scientific evidence is lacking. Soft-rot, tunnelling bacteria and erosion bacteria are able to degrade most hardwoods and softwoods. In addition, tunnelling bacteria have a special ability to degrade species normally regarded as highly resistant to decay. Some timbers have shown more resistance towards decay than others and this natural durability is mainly a result of the chemistry of the actual wood material itself. It is generally found that: 1) Scandinavian softwoods are generally more durable than hardwoods; 2) heartwood is generally more resistant than sapwood; 3) high lignin content and certain wood extracts make the wood more durable; and 4) the most important exception is oak wood, which is very durable in water (Eaton & Hale 1993). In shipbuilding, the varying durability of timbers has been known by experience for a long time and consequently heartwood of oak (*Quercus robur*) and heartwood of pine (*Pinus sylvestris*) are used due to their outstanding qualities.

The toxic effect of oak tannins is believed to obstruct full decay activity by marine fungi and bacteria. Constructions made from oak heartwood are therefore slightly more durable than pine and spruce heartwood timbers, whereas other hardwoods degrade faster (Björdal et al. 1999).

6.6.4 Speed of microbial decay

In the water column the microbial decay process is slow. Analyses of different wreck timbers have shown that oak after 400 years of exposure in the water column is degraded in the outer-most first centimetre, whereas pine is degraded up to depth of 2-4 cm (Björdal & Nilsson 2007). The main degraders were erosion bacteria, while soft-rot decay was only present in the surface layer. It can be assumed that sculptures, made from less durable timbers, generally are more severely degraded.

In marine sediments, the speed of wood decay is even slower, as erosion bacteria are the only active degraders in this near anaerobic environment. Recent re-burial experiments show a penetration of less than 0.1 mm in 3 years at 40 cm depth (Björdal & Nilsson 2008). Viking-Age softwood poles show a decay depth of the sap- and heartwood up to 7 cm after more than 1,000 years in sediments (Björdal et al. 2000).

Today, very little information on microbial decay rates of shipwrecks is available.

6.6.5 Summary

Shipwrecks and submerged wood situated in aquatic environments are attacked and degraded by specialised soft-rot fungi and bacteria despite geographic and local variations in temperature, salinity, nitrogen concentration, and pH. In brackish environments where marine borers are absent, bacteria and soft-rot fungi play a major role in the decomposition of wood. Soft-rot and tunnelling bacteria will soften and degrade the outer wood surface, and erosion bacteria will slowly degrade the interior parts of timbers until only the fragile lignin skeleton remains. Decay takes place even at great depth and below sediments where the decay speed is extremely slow. Today, it is known that the speed of this biological process is mainly dependent on the oxygen concentration in the surrounding water and sediments, but dependent also on the nitrogen concentration as well as wood species and wood properties. The capability of fungi and bacteria to degrade wood in all types of marine, brackish and freshwater environments leads to a permanent on-going process as many different species with supplementary abilities are involved in the process.

7. The decay process of shipwrecks timbers in the Baltic

7.1 General decay processes of wood timbers
Charlotte Gjelstrup Björdal & Christin Appelqvist

Wood degradation takes place in all types of aquatic environments whether saline, brackish, or fresh water, and regardless whether the timbers are situated above or below sediment. The processes that occur, however, are different and primarily it is the rate of wood deterioration that is affected. The consequence is that in some waters, wood constructions of importance for cultural heritage can be preserved for millennia whereas in other environments the same wood will disappear within decades.

Generally, wood constructions situated in all types of sediments degrade extremely slowly compared to wood in the water column. This is mainly due to the very low oxygen concentrations in sediments. For a shipwreck partly covered with sediments, the consequence is that the wood constructions above the seabed are much more degraded than those within the sediment.

Shipworms and gribbles are present in marine waters world-wide and are able to decompose wood within a very short time. Where these organisms are present, only wood that is covered by sediments will remain. Usually, these organisms are not active in brackish- and freshwater environments, and therefore these types of environments are consequently much more protective in regards to wooden wrecks.

The Baltic Sea is an extreme marine environment with salinities ranging from 25 psu at the entrance to the North Sea to 1-2 psu in the innermost parts. Exposed timbers in the southwestern high saline areas are relatively rapidly decomposed, whereas shipwrecks situated in the more brackish areas are preserved for centuries. Shipwrecks exposed in the brackish area (< 8 psu) are generally degraded very slowly, and the decay processes are a combination of microbial activity and physical or mechanical environmental factors. Degrading fungi and bacteria are adapted to wood degradation in both freshwater, brackish water and saline water, which ensure that shipwrecks, wherever they are (rivers, estuaries, lakes, and seas), will slowly decompose as a part of the carbon cycle in nature. The consequences of microbial degradation of timber is a softening of the wood that starts in the outermost layer, which makes the timbers more sensitive to mechanical erosion of the surface, for example, by strong currents and sediment. Microbial degradation and its consequences are described in Chapter 6.6.

This chapter gives an introduction to the complexity and different aspects that could be encountered when evaluating a shipwreck, its depositional environment and the potential threats for its long term preservation *in situ*.

7.2 Decay processes in sediment
Charlotte Gjelstrup Björdal

Degradation of wood exposed in sediment differs in many ways from the decay processes taking place above the seabed, in the seawater column. Most remarkable and outstanding is that the decay process in this environment is extremely slow.

Oxygen concentrations in sediments are very low and the environment is often described as anaerobic. In the upper centimetre of the sediment, the oxygen concentrations decrease from levels similar to the surrounding water into near anaerobic levels (Rasmussen & Jörgensen 1992). The very low oxygen concentrations in the sediments exclude most wood-degrading organisms, and provide therefore favourable preservation conditions for shipwreck timbers. Shipworms might be able to degrade timbers partly covered with sediment, but only if their entrance hole and siphons are above the seabed and there is dissolved oxygen in the sea water. If sediment layers are removed by currents, or contain bottom-dwelling organisms (Ferrari & Adams 1990), the local environment will change around the timbers and become more oxygenated. This will increase the wood degrading processes and endanger the integrity of the construction.

Soft-rot fungi and tunnelling bacteria have been found to degrade wood in the upper few centimetres of the sediment, but are absent at deeper levels. The only wood degradation that continues at greater depths is of bacterial nature and is caused by the so-called erosion bacteria (see Chapter 6.6). These bacteria are able to degrade wood in near anaerobic environments although the process is extremely slow. If timbers are covered by sediment very quickly after becoming submerged, the wood is mainly degraded by erosion bacteria. Such wood has a surprisingly "well-preserved" appearance, and can be found in "mint" condition, archaeologically speaking, and often free of discoloration (**Fig 7.1**). It has been concluded that the degradation process will continue until no more sound wood is available and may go on for thousands of years (Björdal et al. 2000).

Apart from bacterial degradation, wood situated in sediment is also subjected to other processes. Recently, studies using molecular biology showed that archaeological wood could be regarded as a biotope for a wide spectrum of micro-organisms and not only for wood-degrading erosion bacteria (Landy et al. 2008; Helms et al. 2004; Helms 2008). The micro-organisms were present although the wood was totally degraded, and it was suggested that the majority of the bacteria are involved in processes other than decay.

It has been observed that archaeological wood often contains elevated amounts of minerals such as iron and sulphur. The accumulation of sulphur compounds in water-logged archaeological wood has been recently studied through laboratory experiments, and the sulphate-reducing bacteria were found to accumulate sulphur from the environment into degraded parts of wood samples (Fors et al. 2008).

Experiments also indicate that sulphate-reducing bacteria are not true wood degraders but secondary degraders living on breakdown products from erosional bacterial attack. It is highly likely that similar bio-chemical processes control the transformation of other organic and inorganic compounds and involve a wide spectrum of specialised bacteria which could explain the huge consortia of wood-inhabiting bacteria found inside wood.

Recently, monitoring of sediments has been carried out to provide information on on-going bio-geochemical processes (Gregory 2007). Dissolved oxygen content, redox potential, sulphate/sulphide content, organic content and porosity of sediments provide infor-

Fig. 7.1. The sculpture from Kronan *was in mint condition as it was protected by sediments for centuries. It is now on display at Kalmar Länsmuseum in Sweden (photo: R. Lind, Kalmar Länsmuseum).*

mation about the rates of organic turnover and whether it is on-going under oxic or anoxic conditions. However, due to wood being a complex organic material, and that a suite of taxonomically unknown bacteria are responsible for its deterioration, it is currently difficult to correlate explicitly rates of wood deterioration and the environment

As long as shipwreck timbers are protected by sediment, decay will proceed very slowly and also protect the wood from hydrodynamic forces that take place in the water column above the seabed. Thick layers are physically more protective than thin layers, and an experiment in a mar-ine environment showed that a 50 cm-thick layer of sediment was significantly more protective than one 10 cm thick (Björdal & Nilsson 2008).

This indicates that the protective effect of sediment increases with the thickness of the layer. A recent study shows that sandy sediments might be more protective than finer grained sediment with high organic content (Nyström Godfrey et al., in press). Knowledge of the optimal depth of pro-tective sediment or the differences in types of sediments surrounding the wood requires further study.

7.3 Human impact

Martijn Manders & David Gregory

The threat of man to the underwater cultural heritage (UCH) is enormous – one obvious and very much focussed-upon problem is treasure hunting. Indeed, this may cause considerable loss of data and information about our UCH, due to the fact that often archaeological finds are taken away from their contexts without being properly investigated. Afterwards, finds are sold for the benefit of a few and often cannot be traced again for future research (**Fig. 7.2**). Another, maybe even bigger problem is that treasure hunting often attracts a lot of attention from the media, which influences public opinion and presents marine archaeology and UCH in the wrong way. However, other threats may be, at the very least, as de-structive as treasure hunting, especially in relation to the quantity of sites

Fig. 7.2. Wrecks have been subject to commercial salvaging for a long time. Here the tin dredger Karimata *during an attempt to salvage gold from* Lutine (1799) *in the 1930s (collection of Dirk Bruin, Vlieland, the Netherlands).*

being disturbed or even lost. Examples include 1) Sports diving, 2) Fishing, 3) Dredging, 4) Development works, 5) Pollution, 6) Ship movement, and 7) Archaeology.

The negative effects on a site can be diminished by legal and physical protection, good law enforcement and also by raising awareness of the importance of the UCH. Dredging, infra-structural and development works are in many European countries included in the national legislation due to the implementation of the Treaty of Valletta. Therefore during such projects, cultural heritage is, or at least should be, taken into account. Challenging to control are other human effects such as ship movements and pollution because it is difficult to make others responsible for the negative effects on the UCH when the direct impact is problematic to measure and the long-term effects hard to prove.

Although often forgotten, archaeologists themselves may become a threat to the UCH if research is conducted in the wrong way. This may result in immediate deterioration of a site due to sections of a wreck breaking off, trenches being excavated incorrectly, etc. Other threats may lie in the wrong questions being asked while the research is conducted. But effects of archaeological investigation can also be negative in the long term: poorly re-covering a site with sediment or not re-covering a site at all may result in deterioration of material that had previously been stable for centuries.

Some human behaviour may result in damaging the UCH over decades or even hundreds of years. These effects may be taken into consideration when protecting a site *in situ*. One example is climate change, but on a smaller scale this can also be the influence on seabed current patterns of a newly built bridge, shallow-water windmill farm or dyke, which may result in the erosion of newly exposed sites.

Damage to the seabed caused by trawling may be the biggest threat to UCH at the moment (**Fig. 7.3**). Now, due to improved marine geophysical scanning methods we finally understand the scale of seabed disturbance caused by such fishing techniques. This is not so strange when we think of the enormous fishing grounds and the ways fish (especially flat fish and bottom dwelling shellfish) are presently being caught.

Fig. 7.3. Fishing net snagged on the Holland 5 Protected Wreck Site, off southern England, in 2005 (courtesy of Wessex Archaeology for English Heritage).

7.4 Decay rate of shipwrecks

Charlotte Gjelstrup Björdal

General and statistically acceptable information on the decay rate of historical shipwrecks in terms of amount of centimetres or millimetres of wood material degraded per year, decade, or century is not available. But two of the most important factors that influence the speed of decay are well known: the presence or absence of marine borers, and whether the wood is buried in sediment or exposed in the seawater column.

If marine borers are present and timbers are exposed to their activity, total decomposition can take place within decades. But for wrecks situated in the brackish part of the Baltic Sea, decay proceeds very slowly and is mainly caused by the microbial degradation of the wood and the action of physical abrasion, if such forces are present (Björdal & Nilsson 2008). Soft rot is often found restricted to the wood's surface, and penetrates only a few millimetres into submerged wood. This restriction is believed to be related to the lower oxygen concentrations inside the wood, which exclude soft rot from further degradation (Savory 1954; Kohlmeyer & Kohlmeyer 1979).

Only a very few scientific investigations have been undertaken to explore the rate of decay in brackish water, and therefore most of our current knowledge comes from historic shipwrecks. Wood samples taken from three historical shipwrecks, *Vasa, Gröna Jägaren*, and *Riksäpplet*, exposed for about 400 years in the archipelago of Stockholm, show similar decay patterns and rates (Björdal & Nilsson 2007). Decay had progressed less than 1 cm into the oak timbers and up to 4 cm into the pine timbers of these wrecks. All the examined timbers were situated or exposed above the seabed, and none of them were noticeably affected by physical abrasion. Similar decay rates were found in timbers from *Kronan* and *Kraveln*. A newly discovered shipwreck, colloquially known as the "Ghost Ship", contemporary to *Vasa* (1628), was found in international waters in the centre of the Baltic Sea. Preliminary results on the condition of a pine timber from the wreck reveal decay by erosion bacteria to a depth of about 2 cm from the wood's surface (Fors & Björdal 2009). The exposure depth (130 m) appears not to have been more protective than that of wrecks found in shallower waters.

These first studies indicate that soft-rot decay is a superficial related decay form, whereas erosion bacteria degrade the inner parts of shipwreck timbers. Thinner pine wood planks above the seabed are degraded within a few centuries, whereas larger oak timbers might take at least a millennium to degrade. In both cases, the wood's interior is degraded by erosion bacteria which affect the micro structure of the cell wall, but do not totally disintegrate the timber itself (see Chapter 6.6). Carvings on wrecks made from less durable timbers generally have a higher decay rate than structural wood.

Information on wood decay rates in sediment is limited, but experience shows very clearly that wood is in much better condition than when above the seabed (see also Chapter 7.2). Experimental results also indicate a very slow process, where decay rates were far less than 0.1 mm in 3 years at 40 cm beneath the seabed. Two Viking-Age poles excavated from marine sediments were found to be degraded throughout their entire diameter (16 cm) except for a small area in the centre of the heartwood. During the 1,000 years they had been buried, decay had progressed about 7 cm into the wood. The oak hull of *Mary Rose* was examined with a Pilodyn instrument, and decay was found present up to ca. 10-12 mm from the wood's surface. Both soft rot, tunnelling bacteria, and erosion bacteria were found degrading the wood (Mouzouras et al. 1986). Owing to decay by marine borers, only the parts of the hull protected by sediment had survived.

In cases where degraded timbers are also influenced by wave action, strong currents, or sediment erosion, the decay rate is highly increased due to a continuous physical peeling of surface layers of wood. These with time will lead to a complete removal of the wood. Decay rates at such complex sites are very hard to estimate without a closer study of the site.

7.5 Collapse of shipwreck timber structures
Charlotte Gjelstrup Björdal, David Gregory & Martijn Manders

The physical collapse of a shipwreck *in situ* is a complex process, where biological, physical, and also chemical processes interact. Physical collapse is defined here as a collapse of the construction itself where timbers, through the aforementioned processes, are gradually degraded and break away as separate timbers and are either deposited adjacent to the wreck or washed away.

Collapse in saline marine environments

When wood timbers are exposed to marine borers in saline waters, the material is destroyed within a very short time – years rather than decades. The large number of tunnels formed inside the timbers leave behind a fragile skeleton that sooner or later starts to fragment and break up. The shipwreck structures above the sediment will be destroyed simultaneously by the combination of biological degradation and the effects of any water currents present. Only the wood buried in the sediment is protected from this action. When currents and other environmental forces are present in the area, the physical impact on the structure increases and make the degraded timber structures collapse. Loose elements will then be spread by currents. Frequently they can be found close by in re-deposited areas often in what are called scour pits, caused by the effect of currents moving around the upstanding parts of the wreck, as has occurred on the wreck sites of *Mary Rose* and *Invincible* (Quinn et al. 1998; Quinn et al. 1997). In the worst case the wood is transported away and lost from its archaeological context.

Collapse in stable passive brackish environments

For shipwrecks situated in a stable and non-aggressive brackish environment (without strong currents or other potential physical damage and no *Teredo navalis*), wood can remain seemingly intact for a very long time. Decay takes place inside the wood, but is not visible from the outside. Such wood timber looks intact, but may easily break as it has lost its initial strength properties due to microbial decay. The microbial degradation softens the wood, starting in the surface layers, including the openings and joints made when the vessel was built. In addition there will be chemical corrosion around any iron nails and with time the construction will not be able to support itself any longer. The ship might slowly fall apart piece by piece, turning into a puzzle on the seabed.

Collapse in unstable brackish aggressive environments

On the other hand, if a shipwreck is situated in an environment with currents and sediment transport, the hull above the seabed could be exposed to strong physical forces. The situation will be as described above (collapse in stable passive brackish environment), but the process will be faster. The soft wood surface may be peeled off, and ornamentation including tool marks, are destroyed within a relatively short time. This process can be observed on *in situ* wooden carvings where contours slowly "fade" away. As the softened wood around fittings and joints, including holes for iron nails or treenails, are also eroded and removed, timbers will with time be movable and easily affected by physical forces. Strong currents might result in the hull collapsing completely.

8. The spread of shipworm into the Baltic

8.1 Introduction

Christin Appelqvist

The geographical distribution of a species is determined by complex interactions among ecological factors within evolutionary processes. For a shipworm species to expand its present range, the new area needs to meet a minimum set of requirements to support survival of all life stages and reproduction of adults. The environment must fall within the present range of tolerance of all factors affecting the physiology of the organism, such as salinity, temperature, oxygen, and nutrients. Furthermore, the wood habitat must be present and the species have to be capable of surviving predators and competitors in the new environment. Where these basic criteria are met, range expansions are theoretically possible. Many establishments of shipworm into new areas and observed range shifts have been mediated by human activities. A particularly important dispersal vector has been cargo ships used for trade during the 17th to 19th centuries. Larvae in one port have settled onto the hull, become juveniles who have grown to adults, which in turn reproduce, and then release the next generation at the new destination. A new population has then successfully been established in the wooden habitat in the area. In modern times the opening up of geographical barriers of marine routes by channels has facilitated the dispersal of species between oceans. Other possible pathways caused by man today are commercial shipping, which supports the transport of larvae by ballast water, movements of infested recreational wooden boats, and fishing gear. Irrespective of the aid of humans, shipworms have great natural potential for dramatic range shifts due to their highly mobile larval phase. Dispersal of larvae from a spawning source to a settlement site is affected by multiple factors operating at different spatial and temporal scales. It is believed that ocean currents are the determining factor controlling dispersal, and it is tempting to assume that tiny shipworm larvae act as passive particles in strong hydrographical forces. However, recent research on other marine invertebrates suggests that larval behaviour, like vertical migration, can influence where they will end up. More investigation of the behaviour of shipworm larvae is necessary to understand these processes better.

The spread of *Teredo navalis* in the Baltic is dynamic, and to determine the distribution range requires surveys on a regular basis that also include areas free from attacks. Reduction and expansion of the species range happens all the time. Questions to be considered when setting the limit are: how long must a species have been locally extinct to say it is a range contraction, and when an individual is observed beyond its range limit does that mean the range has expanded? To determine the range for an animal like shipworm that deposits calcareous tubes in wood and destroys its habitat might make it easier to study, compared to organisms that do not leave traces behind, even if it is hard to detect living specimens of shipworm inside wood. However, the presence of a centuries-old wooden wreck is clear evidence that shipworms have not been highly active in that specific area. Finding calcified tubes inside a wooden wreck does not say anything about when the attack occurred or whether there is an active (i.e. living) shipworm population in the geographical area. To determine this, living specimens must be found either by pulling waterlogged wood apart or by detecting extruded siphons at the wood object's surface.

To understand the causes and consequences of geographical range shift of *Teredo navalis* in the Baltic Sea, new records can be compared with existing range data that are both accurate and complete. In this chapter we summarise the reported outbreaks within the Baltic Sea region since the late 19th century followed by new results of a modelling study.

8.2 Shipworm: an old story of trouble

Martijn Manders & Vincent de Bruyn

In the past, and even now, mankind has suffered extensively from the ravages of shipworm. Ships, pilings, embankments, dykes, and all other wooden constructions in the marine environment suffer the attack of the infamous shipworm. Among others, Aristotle, Ovid and Pliny write about the problems of shipworm around the Mediterranean. The Romans would use thin lead sheets to protect their ships, Columbus had problems with marine borers, and Venice tried to find solutions for the problem by sending people to China. The many problems that shipworm has caused in the past has resulted in a substantial list of methods and means to try to combat them. The Netherlands, in particular, has suffered greatly from the effects of shipworm. Shipworm infestations in the Netherlands are recorded in 1730-33, 1770, 1827 and 1858-59. The shipworm infestation in the 1730s may have been the most disastrous, causing great concern amongst the Dutch population. Shipworms were present in such large numbers that they managed to destroy all dykes, embankments and sluice gates.

Before the 1730s there was no mention of such a plague. However, shipworms were already known. As early as 1720, texts mention Dutch ships and (harbour) poles that were eaten by marine borers.

That shipworm was the talk of the day has to do with the fear of floods. Indeed, large parts of the Netherlands were – and still are – under sea level. Pilings, dykes and embankments were so heavily attacked by marine borers – the attacks could occur within a few months – that the strength of the levees was compromised. It is therefore not surprising that people started to look for a scapegoat to this problem and this was found in the form of homosexuals. In the years 1730, 1931 and 1932, 82 men were sentenced to death just because of their sexual preference. It should be noted that this persecution was not just because of the shipworm epidemic, they were also being blamed for a serious epidemic among cattle that occurred at the same time.

The shipworm epidemic of the 1730s was well documented and archival material is preserved to this day. Other problems with shipworm attacks in 1858 and 1859 are also well documented. However, the effects of these attacks seem to have been far less than the attack in 1730.

Ships have also been greatly affected by shipworm, especially in the warm tropical and sub-tropical waters where the vessels of many European nations sailed during the Age of Discovery. For example, Christopher Columbus, during his fourth voyage in 1502, experienced a near catastrophe: near Panama the ships *Gallega* and *Vizcaína* were lost due to damage caused by shipworm.

In 1649 the Dutch Admiral Witte de With encountered the same problems in Brazil with his fleet and had to replace the shells (planking) of his ships.

There are many reports that shipworms were first transported to European waters on the ships of the Dutch East Indian Company (VOC) during the 17th and 18th centuries. This may be true, but it is also clear that they were already present in Northern European waters before this time, as attested by the writings of classical scholars. Furthermore, fossils of shipworms have been found in Belfast, London, and Brussels dating from the Eocene (56-34 million years ago). Great problems arising after 1730 are probably due to more favourable climatic conditions for the reproduction and survival of shipworms, thus causing an explosion of the population.

Throughout the centuries there have been many methods devised and tested to protect wooden constructions in the marine environment from the ravages of shipworm. The success of some of these methods is well documented, whereas others are not so well described. Several writers in the 18th and 19th centuries describe the methods and tools that were used to strengthen and protect the embankments and dykes in the Netherlands. When reviewing the literature, it is striking that most books are written just after a shipworm infestation. Thus, writers like Rousset, Massuet, and Sellius wrote books in 1733, at the end of the shipworm infestation from 1730 and this trend repeats itself (**Fig. 8.1**). In 1771, David Meese wrote a book just after a shipworm infestation, as did Vrolik in 1860. Amongst the preventative methods these authors describe are the building of additional dams to reinforce the dykes, building reinforcement

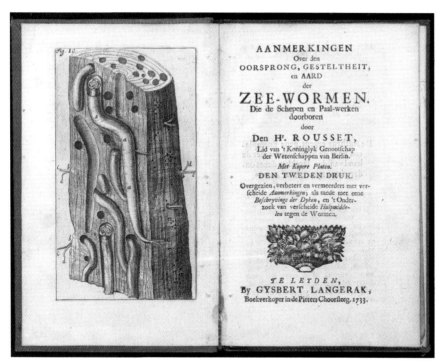

Fig. 8.1. J. Rousset de Missy, 1733. Aanmerkingen over den oorsprong, gesteltheit, en aard der zee-wormen die de schepen en paal-werken doorboren (Leiden, Gysbert Langerak).

seaweed dykes, using poison, and covering pilings with tar, pitch, harpics, and leaded chalk.

There were even other methods applied: In the 18th century in Toulon large quantities of oak sawdust were used in an attempt to poison ship-worms.

Around 1860, the woodwork in Monnickendam and Edam (two villages on the shores of the Zuiderzee in the Netherlands) was relatively little affected by shipworm, while other villages had a lot of damage. It was dis-covered that this was probably due to the polluted waters of these areas: the two cities had an extensive herring and anchovy industry and its waste was dumped into the surrounding waters.

David Meese (1771), like Rousset and Massuet (1733), also writes about using substances that could be applied to pilings and wood exposed to seawater and shipworm. Amongst these techniques is a mixture that consists of tar, pitch, and crushed glass or lime, which is painted on to the wood. Another remedy is the use of a mixture of arsenic and Spanish green (an old copper oxide pigment). However, once dried this substance would "peel off" the poles when they were driven into the seabed, thus giving access to the shipworm larvae . Even if it would stay on when the poles were being driven into the seabed, it was then beaten off by the waves afterwards. A further mixture consisting of linseed oil, resin, and turpentine was seen not to work as, when this was exposed to the heat of the sun, it melted and ran off the wood. Massuet, Rousset, and Meese were not the only authors to write about the application of toxic substances to pilings, piers, locks, and ships; amongst others, Des Landes (1737), Venema (1865), Baumhauer (1866), and Redeke (1912) did so, too. These many different, often not (long-)lasting agents have not only been used on the surface of poles. Sometimes holes were drilled into the wood in order to pour the substances inside, a technique which Rousset already notes as not working. Meese states that the poles where these methods were applied even deteriorated faster and more extensively than others. This was likely caused by the man-made holes, which made it easier for marine borers to get into the wood.

Another method described by Meese (1771) to protect wood pilings was to make a wooden structure, called a "skirt", which went around the outside of the pole. The pole and the inside of the skirt were smeared with a (toxic) substance, and the space between the pole and the skirt was filled with cow hair. This method wasn't really effective, either: the outside of the skirt was still exposed unprotected to seawater, and thus became a suitable home for marine borers. After some time, the skirt no longer protected the pole as it too was degraded, and the skirt, along with the cow hair and the (toxic) substance were washed away.

Cow hair was also used to protect ships: cow hair and tar were put between layers of shell planking (and also specially applied to fine pine wood doubling, or outer planking). Another way of protecting wooden poles was the use of iron, in particular iron nails (and later steel, copper, or iron plates). Iron nails were hammered into the wood and on exposure to sea water would corrode, creating an impermeable layer of rust on the surface of the wood. This was not only applied to ships: for example, in 2003 in Zeeland (the southwestern province of the Netherlands), two heavy pine poles that were full of nail holes and impressions of nail heads were found.

The double layer of shell planking and/or shell planking with a thin extra layer of pine wood on the exterior (the cladding) was applied to ships for several reasons. Indeed – in combination with the iron nails and cow hair – it slowed down the attack, but the outer layer of planking being attacked by shipworm was not devastating, but was actually calculated. It was the inner shell planking that was important. That layer needed to be protected at all costs, because it made the ship stay afloat. If this layer was attacked then the whole ship was lost. The other shell layers were replaceable, so this is what was done. After each voyage, the thin sacrificial layer of pine on the outside of East Indiamen were replaced with a new layer – it was a sacrificial layer and therefore not part of the real ship construction.

The ultimate solution found to protect the wood used in dykes and embankments was simple but very expensive: replace/reinforce dykes and embankments with stones. These stones were specially imported from the Netherlands, Germany, Denmark, and Norway (**Fig. 8.2**).

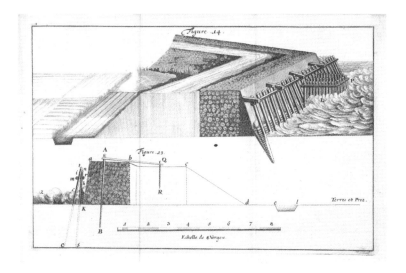

Fig. 8.2. Wierdijk, as described by Rousset. Universiteitsbibliotheek Amsterdam (UvA) Bijzondere collecties, OT O 63- 1265, Rousset, 1733.

Fig. 8.3. Drawing of marine borers from the 1700s. Universiteitsbibliotheek Amsterdam (UvA) Bijzondere collecties, OT O 63- 1265, Rousset, 1733.

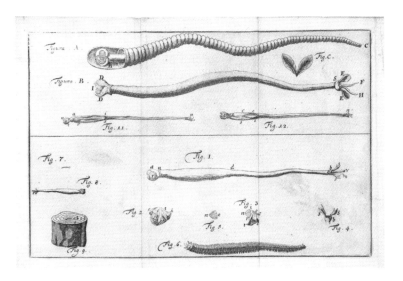

The methods to protect ships against shipworm can be divided into three categories: 1) The coating or covering of a vessel with a substance/material that stops shipworm larvae settling on the "superstructure" of the ships timbers; 2) Treating the vessels so that marine borers will die if they already are present; 3) Replacement and repair of ships that were greatly affected by the presence of shipworm.

1) The covering of ships was a common practice in the past. One of the methods was the use of cladding (doubling), effectively adding an extra layer of wood on top of the actual structural timbers of the ship. This cladding, often of pine or spruce, served as a sacrificial layer to protect the ship's structural timbers. Shipworm settled on the cladding and destroyed it, and when it was badly damaged, it was replaced. There is also evidence that double layers of shell planking were also used but not necessarily to protect solely against shipworm but also for protection against ice and ordnance, but also to give added strength and stability. Examples of the use of double shell planking include *Mauritius* (wrecked 1609), *Batavia* (wrecked 1629), *Avondster* (wrecked 1659) and *Utrecht* (wrecked 1648); these vessels were all active in the tropics and a third layer of cladding was also observed. Among other ships with a double layer of shell planking applied for different reasons are the Scheurrak SO1 wreck (wrecked 1593) and the B&W 1 wreck (a Dutch "*verlanger*" or extended ship). *Mauritius* also had an extra layer of lead between the outer and inner cladding and there are several other references to this practice in the Netherlands, France, and England. Another method was to use tar and cow hair between the layers of planking and the cladding.

2) Several methods have been applied to treat ships to kill shipworm that had already become established in the wood. Often ships were pulled out of the water, and with a reed or straw the hull was carefully burned. The shell of the ship was "roasted", killing the worms. The boat still was damaged by shipworm, but the attack was stopped. Ships were also sailed into the freshwater rivers of large estuaries and, since shipworm only lives in salt water, infestations could be stopped.

3) If the extent of attack was not too great, damaged parts would often be replaced. This was only done in the cases where it was economically viable. We can include the doubling of the skin/shell planking as one of these methods. Indeed, the sacrificial hull layer was replaced every time a ship returned from a long voyage.

Conclusion

Many different ingenious methods have been applied to prevent or repair damage caused by shipworm in the past. Many methods are no longer applicable due to the toxicity of the substances used. Other methods, such as the use of a skirt or a sacrificial hull layer, are still useful but may not be applicable to cultural and historical sites preserved *in situ*. This section has focused on the Netherlands, where the problems with *Teredo navalis* have been an on-going struggle for centuries (**Fig. 8.3**). The solutions have been not only amusing, but they also show us how much impact the threat and the actual damage can have on a society. Hopefully, the Baltic Sea will be spared from the battle against shipworm.

8.3 The spread of shipworm into the Baltic: a brief history
David Gregory & *Christin Appelqvist*

Outbreaks of shipworm have occurred throughout the past 100 years or more in Danish territorial waters and the southern Baltic – it is not just a recent phenomenon. Recent reports from 1990 to 2009 state that these attacks appear to be worsening or are unprecedented. Many publications consider the reasons for the spread of *Teredo navalis* and several hypotheses for the causes of this spreading have been proposed (Møhlenberg 2002):

- Invasive species spread in ships' ballast water
- The marine/water environment in and around the Baltic is less polluted
- Poorer quality wood used in marine constructions which is more vulnerable to attack
- Periodic influx of high salinity water into the Baltic. This is related to the meteorological phenomenon called the North Atlantic Oscillation, as discussed in Chapter 4
- Higher than average summer temperatures in Baltic waters

Outbreaks of *Teredo navalis* along the Baltic coast of Germany have been a reoccurring event since at least 1872, with records in almost each decade since then. In 1938, Becker claims the eastern limit of attacks to be at Zingst (review in Clapp & Kenk 1963). Also in Danish waters, attack by *Teredo navalis* in inner Danish waters has been fluctuating over the last 100 years; large outbreaks have been seen in several periods during 1924-1926, 1932-1935, 1937-1941, 1947-1950, and 1955-1960. In the 1970s and 1980s there was a dearth of literature relating to attacks, but in the 1990s problems seemed to start again. Extensive infestations occurred between 1993-1996 along the coast of Mecklenburg-Western Pomerania, as far east as Hiddensee (Sordyl et al. 1998). It was also reported that in 1997 shipworm had spread around Sleswig in southern Germany and in southern Jutland. Due to better living conditions, *Teredo navalis* has spread further east in the Baltic Sea.

The requirement of relatively high salinity in order to survive has kept the Baltic Sea safe from attack by shipworm. Periodical attacks in 2-3 year spells have been reported along the western-most stretches of the Baltic coast of Germany, but viable populations of shipworm had never arisen until the 1990s, when, according to German authorities, almost €10 million of damage was done to wooden structures along the coast of Mecklenburg-West Pomerania over a five-year period.

The presence of shipworm in the Baltic is limited to Germany, Denmark and the southern-most part of Sweden. It has spread north to Ruegen

Island. Further spread is not possible due to low salinity. Some anecdotal cases mention the occurrence of shipworm along the southwestern Polish coast of the Baltic Sea. This is likely due to the occurrence of drifting timbers. The infested timbers might travel as far as the Lithuanian coast, but no living shipworms are found inside the timber. The spread of shipworm to the inner Baltic remains to be determined.

Apart from reports of the spread and attack of shipworm, there appear to be various reasons for its spread and the two factors that stand out are higher than average summer water temperatures and periodic influx of high saline water from the Kattegat. Kristensen (1969) carried out an extensive study looking at shipworm attack between 1900 and 1967, attempting to correlate it with surface temperature and salinity. Kristensen concludes that only high summer temperatures and attacks correlate and that there are many reasons to be cautious when interpreting the data due to the many other influential parameters. Møhlenberg (2002) shows that in years when attacks were reported, average water temperatures were higher than 17°C as opposed to 15.7°C in years without attacks. Møhlenberg also introduces the idea that apart from higher than average summer temperatures there is a correlation between winter storms and western winds. These occur as a result of a large air pressure difference between Iceland and the Azores – the so called North Atlantic Oscillation index (NAO). This phenomenon can lead to inflows of highly saline and oxygenated water from the North Sea. These events are termed Major Baltic Inflows (MBI) – they are of episodic character and are the only mechanisms by which the central Baltic deep water is renewed. Although the cycle of water renewal has been well documented, the meteorological and oceanographic processes controlling this in the Baltic are still not totally understood (Schinke & Matthäus 1998). Nevertheless, it does appear that these inflows are characterised by two phases. The first is high pressure over the Baltic region with easterly winds, followed by several weeks of strong zonal wind and pressure fields over the North Atlantic and Europe. Several large inflows have been documented in the past (**Fig. 8.4**).

The decreasing frequency and intensity of major inflows since the mid-1970s and their complete absence from 1983 to 1993 is explained by Schinke and Matthäus (1998) as being due to increased zonal circulation linked with intensified precipitation in the Baltic region and increased river run-off to the Baltic during this period. It is interesting to note that some of the outbreaks of shipworm, as recorded from the documentary evidence, do coincide with these large incursions and may warrant further investigation – certainly for the periods from 1980 to the present.

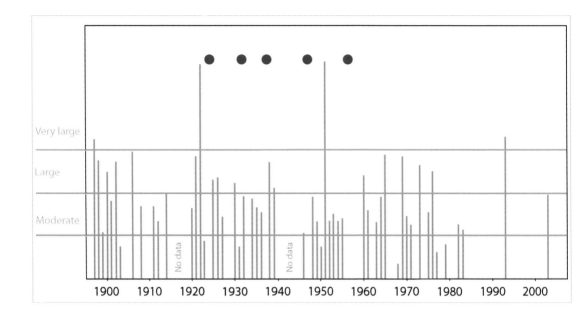

Fig. 8.4. Major Baltic Inflows from 1880 (modified after Schinke & Matthäus 1989; Meier &Gustafsson 2009). The red dots show the times when a shipworm attack has been recorded, according to the literature discussed in Chapter 8.3.

8.4 Where are they today?

Christin Appelqvist

To our knowledge, the most eastern area of reported attacks by ship-worms in the Baltic Sea is at Hiddensee, north-west of the German island of Ruegen. During the years 1993-1996 a comprehensive investigation was carried out along the German coast of Mecklenburg-Western Pomerania (Sordyl et al. 1998). No attacks were found at Dranske north of Ruegen, or at three locations close to Usedom near the border to Poland.

The most recent study of the distribution of shipworms along the Swedish coast and around the island Bornholm (DK) was conducted between the years 2005-2009 in water depths of 0.5-2 m (Appelqvist, forthcoming). Wood panels were submerged in 13 harbours from the Norwegian border in the north to Ystad in the south and five additional harbours around Bornholm. Infestation occurred in all panels on the west coast down to Klagshamn south of Malmö. No attacks were found during this time along the southern coast between Falsterbo to Ystad. No attacks were found in wood panels from the harbours around Bornholm. In general all other coastal waters of Denmark, except part of the eastern coast of Zealand (south of Copenhagen to the island of Møn), seem to be target waters of attack by shipworms.

8.5 A new GIS tool for the detection of "Hot Spot" areas
Zyad Al Hamdani & Christin Appelqvist

Geographic Information Systems (GIS) software is becoming widely used in different aspects of life. It is an important and valuable analytical tool in many challenges we face in the world today, ranging from global climate changes to social and human studies. GIS is a mapping technology that allows the user to create and interact with a variety of maps and data sources. GIS integrates databases with geo-referenced spatial data (maps tied to specific known locations) – in other words, GIS allows the user to create visual displays of tabular information. In GIS the user is able to decide how data will be displayed. The need for such a system arose from the fact that:
1) 70% of information has a geographic component, making spatial analysis an essential tool
2) The ability to assimilate divergent sources of data, both spatial and non-spatial (attribute data)
3) Visualisation impact
4) Analytical capability
5) Sharing of information

What aids such growth in GIS applications is the development in Information and Communication Technology, rapidly declining cost of computers, the impact of visual presentation of projects (a picture is worth a thousand words), and geographical features and the data describing them are part of our everyday life – most of our daily decisions are somehow geographically oriented.

One of the main applications of GIS is in the field of the natural sciences as it is closely related to the spatially distributed variables that constitute the basic parameters in any research work in this branch of the sciences.

In the **WreckProtect** project, the GIS tools were used extensively. In fact processing data and producing the required maps would take a much longer period if it was performed by conventional methods. The reason for that is the large amount of data to be handled and processed for each map-production endeavour. The Baltic Sea environmental parameters were used for the **WreckProtect** project to produce maps that show the spatial and temporal variation of different algebraic combinations of these parameters. The environmental parameters have been obtained from DHI Water, Environment, Health (*http://www.dhigroup.com*). These parameters are the monthly averaged modelled datasets of salinity, temperature, and oxygen content for both the upper and lower layers of the Baltic Sea. DHI uses a regional climate model in their MIKE 3 numerical modelling system for 3D flows to produce a nested grid setup with 9 nautical miles horizontal resolution in the Baltic Sea and 3 nautical miles for the seas around Denmark (**Fig. 8.5**). More information on the modelling process can be found in the DHI/Denmark website. The modelled datasets of the environmental parameters cover two periods; the hindcast datasets for the period 1980-2008 and the predicted period from 2009-2020. The model was calibrated for the first 10 years of the hindcast period and validated for the remaining period. Model calibration means the adjustment of the model until it compares well with the observed data. The model is validated by checking if the model compares equally well with other sets of data without any further adjustment. A number of monitoring stations spatially distributed in the Baltic Sea were used in the model calibration (**Fig. 8.6**).

Research in the **WreckProtect** project partially focused on studying the influence of the abovementioned abiotic parameters on the distribution of the shipworm *Teredo navalis*. The minimum tolerance limit for both the adults and the larvae was presented (**Table 8.1**). These limits were used in a GIS model that combines the previously mentioned parameters to produce spatial extension maps of the combined parameters. The "*Teredo Scenario I*" is the minimum tolerance limits for larval metamorphism and adult reproduction and "*Teredo scenario II*" only represent possible reproduction of adults (shown in **Table 8.1**).

Maps were produced for the first 9 m of the upper water layer (for the larvae distribution), and maps were also produced for the bottom water layer (the adult distribution). The datasets were compiled in one database, restructured and divided into monthly average ASCII files of grid points with geographic locations and environment parameter values. A total of 3,936 files were produced from the database. These represent 41 years (1980-2020), 12 months average, and 6 datasets (three for the top water layer and three for the bottom water layer). To work with such a large amount of datasets, a geo-processing GIS tool called ModelBuilder was utilised. Geo-processing is based on a framework of data transformation, where the input dataset can be visualised on the same platform

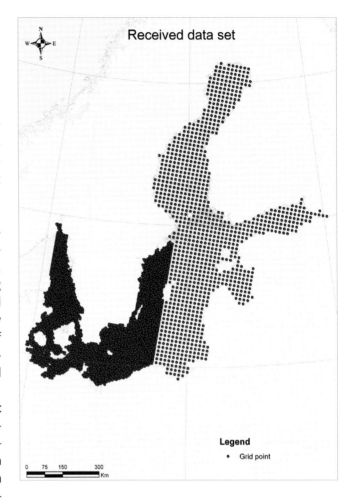

Fig. 8.5. Spatial distribution of the environmental parameters.

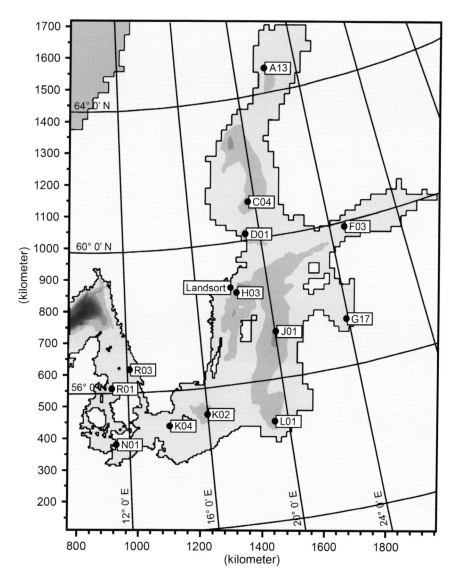

Fig. 8.6. Measuring stations used to calibrate the model.

Table 8.1. Lowest tolerance limits for three environmental parameters used as classification criteria for the Teredo Scenarios in the GIS model.
a) Scenario I: possible reproduction by adults and metamorphosis of larvae.
b) Scenario II: possible reproduction by adults.

Parameter	a) Scenario I	b) Scenario II
Temperature (°C)	≥ 12	≥ 11
Salinity (PSU)	≥ 8	≥ 8
Oxygen (mg O_2/l)	≥ 4	≥ 4

before and after the application of a geo-process such as gridding. Data analysis, data conversion, and management are some basic tools in the geo-processing. An enormous amount of applications are available for the GIS software which can effectively enhance the interpretation and final presentation of the data.

Geo-processing can be performed in four different ways: it can be accessed through the tool box, it can be interactively typed in the command line window, used in script environment such as the programming language Python, or can be worked with in ModelBuilder to build a GIS task-based workflow (**Fig. 8.7**).

Performing geo-processing through ModelBuilder is an effective and robust way of handling all these datasets in one integrated form. Model-Builder enables the automation of the work flow in the geo-processing operation by stringing processes together in the model diagram that will execute in sequence when the model is run. This reduces the processing time considerably, especially in complex models where a large number of geo-processing operations are performed.

An example of a GIS ModelBuilder is shown in **Fig. 8.8**. It is composed of an input dataset in XYZ format (ASCII), a "variable" geo-processing tool which can be altered according to the required operation, and the output dataset. Input datasets can be added and processed in a batch mode. There can be as many tools as required, and the output of each operation can be visually inspected so errors can be spotted and corrected during processing.

For the **WreckProtect** project three types of models were constructed by ModelBuilder: the first (the fundamental model) is to combine

Fig. 8.7. The four geo-processing methods in ArcGIS.

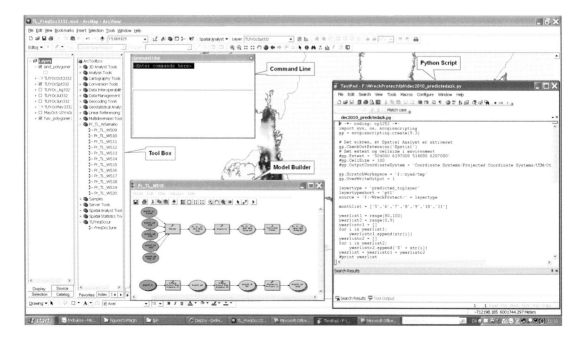

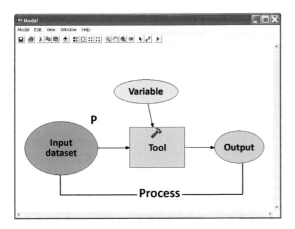

Fig. 8.8. The ModelBuilder diagram.

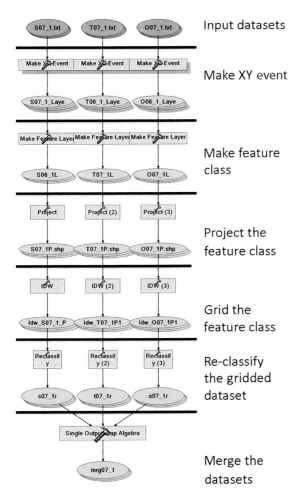

Fig. 8.9. Example of the fundamental model showing various stages of geo-processing.

the environmental parameters for individual months of each year, the second is to deduce the maximum spatial extension of each combination on a yearly basis, and the third is to calculate the frequency of occurrence of the combined parameters of each month over the hindcast and the predicted periods.

The diagram shown in **Fig. 8.9** represents the fundamental model where each processing stage is briefly explained. The datasets of all 12 months and of all parameters (here Salinity, Temperature, and Oxygen for the year 2009 are shown) were loaded in the model at the primary stage. The geo-processing tools were added subsequently to the model with their variables set to the required output. First the projection of the datasets has to be defined as well as the interpolation process for gridding, the reclassification thresholds, and the merging conditions. These parameters can be readily fed to the model during the building stage. The model is validated first to check for error and to synchronise data variables. The final stage is running the model which yields the merged environmental parameters for each month of the year 2009. All processing stages can be visually inspected during the model execution, and that reduces the processing time as errors can be spotted and corrected and the model can resume from the last stage it reached without having to start all over again.

The output from these fundamental models is a raster that can be loaded into ArcMap and classi-

fied according to the different combinations of the environmental parameters already presented above in **Table 8.1**. The resulting classified
raster shows the spatial extension of each parametric combination a
particular month of a particular year. The extension of the "*Teredo
Scenarios*" represents the "Hot Spots", representing where extra care
must be taken for the shipwrecks or submerged wooden constructions
in that region. The model can be exported to other users and run as
many times as required; variables can be changed according to
the required output and geo-processes can be added or removed from
the model without affecting the operations that were performed in the
previous stage.

8.6 Risk of spread: modelling results

Christin Appelqvist & Zyad Al Hamdani

Species distributions are in constant flux and alter in space and through
time. To determine the range size or the risk of spread in the future is a
difficult task and a great challenge. Within the EU funded-project **Wreck-
Protect** we address the following questions with the aim to predict the
risk of spread of *Teredo navalis* in the Baltic Sea for the period 2009-2020.
Will a modelled favourable scenario for *Teredo navalis* occur more or
less frequently in the near future (2009-2020) compared with the past
30 years (1980-2008) in the area between Skagerrak to Bothnia Bay? If
so, how much of each parameter contributes to this change? Will some
months differ more than others? Based on the GIS modelling process of
the two "Teredo Scenarios" (described above in Chapter 8.5), the following results were obtained.
    The study area Skagerrak to Bothnia Bay exhibits a significant temporal
and spatial variation in the occurrence of the *Teredo Scenarios* in both the
top and bottom layer.

Results of Scenario I (possible larval metamorphosis and adult reproduction in the top layer)

Scenario I occurs in the top layer from May until October and is totally
absent during the winter months November-April, based on monthly average of the parameters (**Figs. 8.10-8.21**). In May Scenario I mainly occurs
in shallow areas close to the coast of Denmark and Germany (**Figs. 8.10,
8.16**). In June the water temperature rises and the scenario criteria are
met in all years in the Kattegat and the Sounds and occasionally in Skagerrak (**Figs. 8.11, 8.17**). From July-September an almost uniform pattern
is shown over the whole Skagerrak and Kattegat area for both hindcast
and predicted modelled data (**Figs. 8.12-8.14, 8.18-8.20**). A gradient is

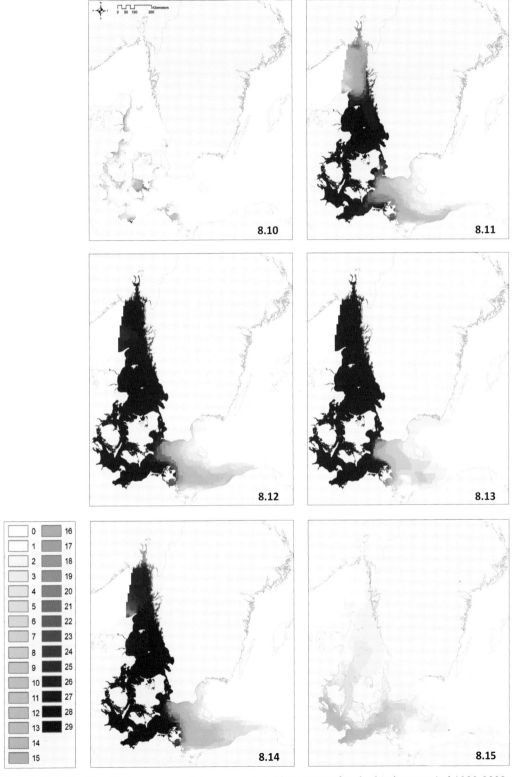

Figs. 8.10-8.15. *Monthly frequency of the occurrence of Scenario I for the hindcast period 1980-2008.*

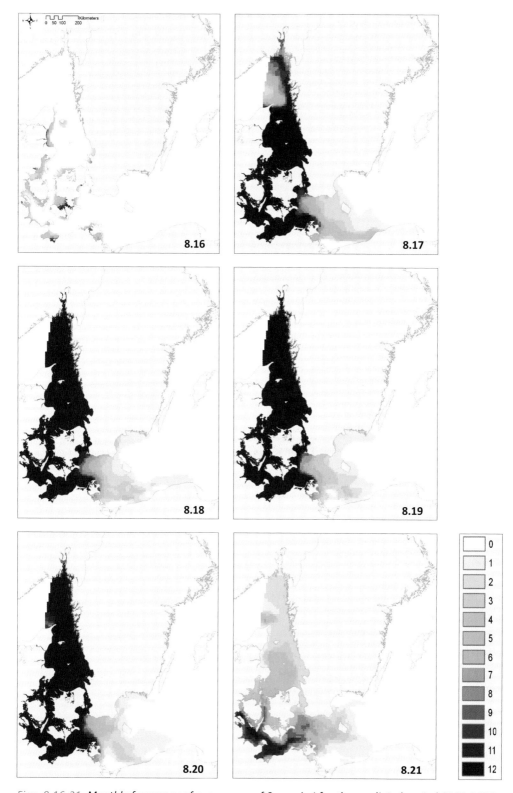

Figs. 8.16-21. Monthly frequency of occurrence of Scenario I for the predicted period 2009-2020.

shown in the southern Baltic, and east and north from here up to Bothnia Bay the salinity is too low and the scenario is totally absent. In October the water temperature decreases, and the model shows great variation between years in the study area (**Figs. 8.15, 8.21**). In Skagerrak and Kattegat Scenario I is totally absent in the hindcast period 1980-1999 (**Figs. 8.22-8.23**). However, an increasing frequency of occurrence of Scenario I for the predicted data is noticed over the whole study area (**Fig. 8.25**). This trend is visible already in the first decade of the 21th century (**Fig. 8.24**).

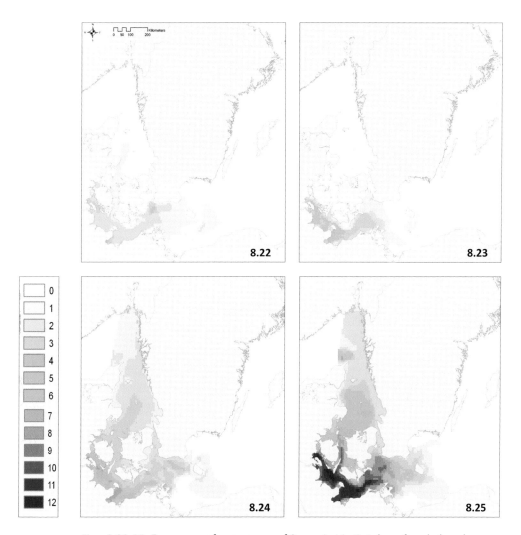

Figs. 8.22-25. *Frequency of occurrence of Scenario I in October of each decade.*

Results of Scenario II (possible reproduction of adults in the bottom layer)

Scenario II appears for the first time in May in shallow areas (**Figs. 8.26, 8.33**). The presence of the scenario increases subsequently during the summer months and it occurs with high frequency until October (**Figs. 8.27-8.31, 8.34-8.38**). The scenario is still most frequent in shallow coastal areas, in waters less than 15 m deep in the Kattegat, around Darss Sill, and in the Western Arkona basin. In contrast to Scenario I, where the top layer is totally devoid of the scenario in November, Scenario II first disappears one month later (**Figs. 8.32, 8.39**). This is because the surface water is affected by the colder overlaying air layer and consequently is cooling down faster than the deep water. It is in October and November when the water temperature rises to ≥11° C and Scenario II is visible in the deepest bottom layers (**Figs. 8.31-8.32, 8.38-8.39**). There is no large difference in the frequency of occurrence of the modelled Scenario II between hindcast and predicted years (**Figs. 8.40-8.41**).

A spatial analysis of the modelled data of the two water layers showed no obvious difference in the geographical distribution of the scenarios between hindcast and predicted years (**Figs. 8.40-8.43**). However, the spatial extent of the combined environmental conditions represented by the *Teredo Scenarios* show a wider range in the model than where shipworm attack has been reported in reality. Consequently, this model has to be validated, supplied with more parameters, and the accuracy of the *Teredo Scenarios* for the Baltic *Teredo* population need to be determined.

The conclusions of these results are that there is a higher risk of spread of *Teredo navalis* in the top water layer of the Baltic Sea during the coming decade due to prolongation of the infestation season but not due to range extension. The risk is highest in southern Denmark and western Germany. As mentioned above in Chapter 6.2, the spawning of *Teredo navalis* is stimulated and controlled by sea temperature. This shipworm species is tremendously prolific. Each female spawns three or four times in a season. Therefore, a prolongation of the warmer period might lead to additional spawning events. More larvae will then have the opportunity to settle onto a wooden wreck. Fur-

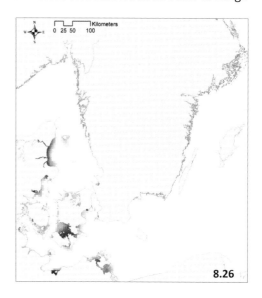

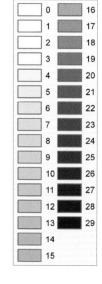

8.26

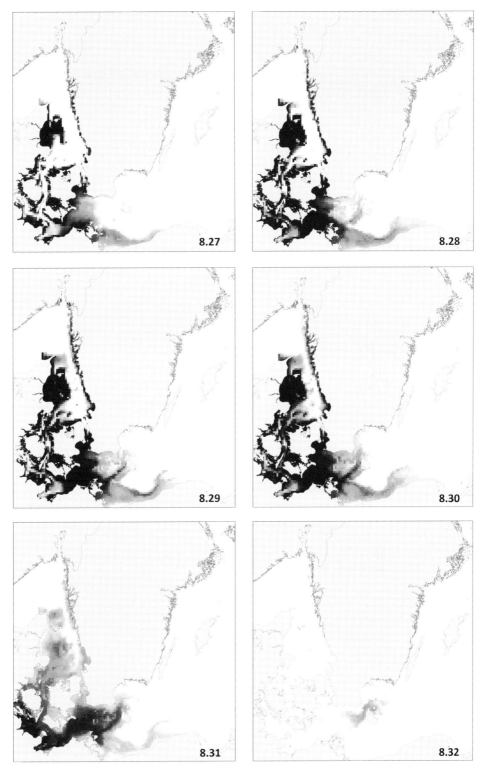

Figs. 8.26-32. (starting on facing page) Monthly frequency of occurrence of Scenario II for the hindcast period 1980-2008.

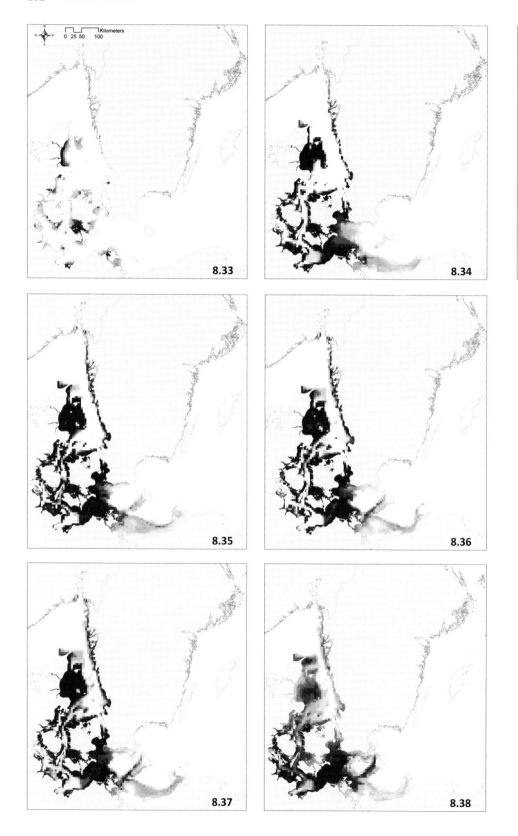

8.39

Figs. 8.33-39. *(left, and starting on facing page) Monthly frequency of occurrence of Scenario II for the predicted period 2009-2020.*

Fig. 8.40. *(below) Monthly frequency of occurrence of Scenario I for the hindcast period 1980-2008 over all years.*

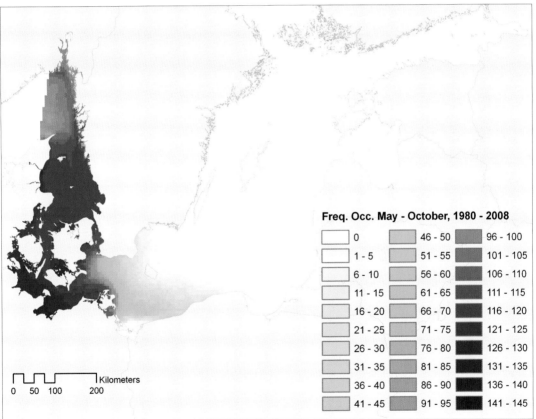

Freq. Occ. May - October, 1980 - 2008

0		46 - 50		96 - 100	
1 - 5		51 - 55		101 - 105	
6 - 10		56 - 60		106 - 110	
11 - 15		61 - 65		111 - 115	
16 - 20		66 - 70		116 - 120	
21 - 25		71 - 75		121 - 125	
26 - 30		76 - 80		126 - 130	
31 - 35		81 - 85		131 - 135	
36 - 40		86 - 90		136 - 140	
41 - 45		91 - 95		141 - 145	

Kilometers
0   50   100   200

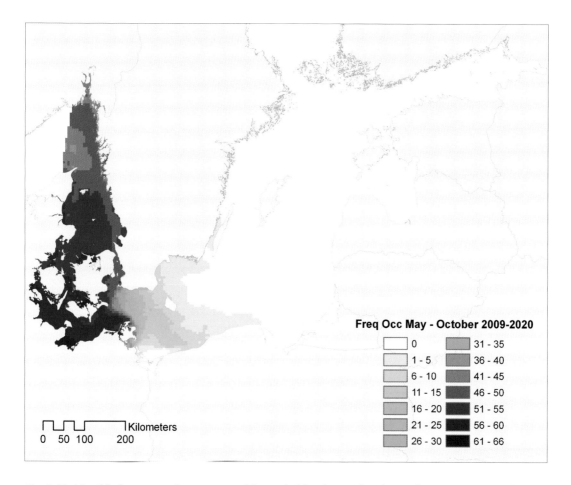

Fig. 8.41. Monthly frequency of occurrence of Scenario I for the predicted period 2009-2020 over all years.

thermore, since the growth rate is also highly temperature dependent, the damage by each individual every year might be more extensive in the future. More successful shipworm recruits will have the chance to grow from juveniles to adults within a season. Since the adults are less susceptible and can survive the winter period better than a juvenile, the risk of establishment of new meta-populations will be higher.

Exactly how *Teredo navalis* will react to climate change and new environmental conditions is impossible to answer, since the Baltic population has never faced this scenario. However, at present this model is the best available. More experimental research is needed to understand how *Teredo navalis* will react to higher temperature but lower salinity. Other questions include: How will this species respond to new pH levels in the future? Will more areas in the Baltic Sea be free from oxygen, and how will that affect degradation of shipwrecks?

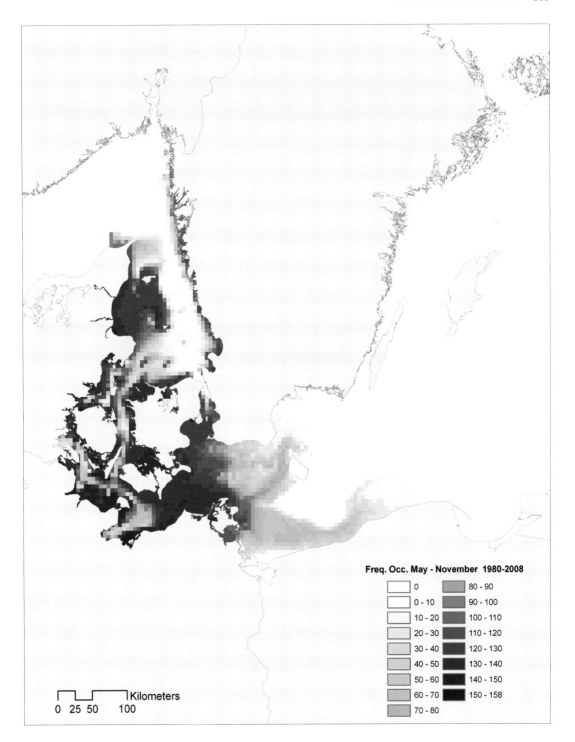

Fig. 8.42. *Monthly frequency of occurrence of Scenario II for the hindcast period 1980-2008 over all years.*

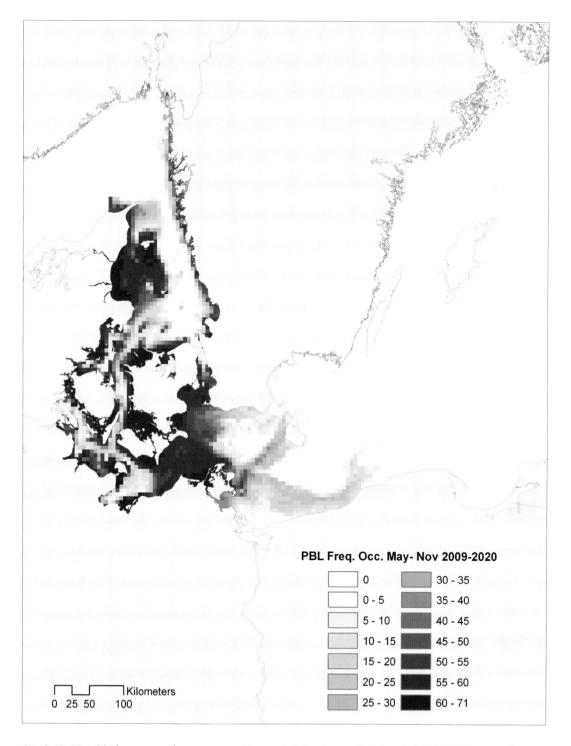

PBL Freq. Occ. May- Nov 2009-2020

0	30 - 35
0 - 5	35 - 40
5 - 10	40 - 45
10 - 15	45 - 50
15 - 20	50 - 55
20 - 25	55 - 60
25 - 30	60 - 71

0 25 50   100 Kilometers

Fig. 8.43. Monthly frequency of occurrence of Scenario II for the predicted period 2009-2020 over all years.

9. *In-situ* preservation of a wreck site

David Gregory & Martijn Manders

9.1 Introduction

Underwater archaeology is still a relatively young discipline, starting effectively in the 1940s with the advent of the aqualung. In the following 40-50 years several underwater shipwreck sites have been excavated, raised, conserved and exhibited in northwest Europe: notably the Viking-Age ships from Skuldelev (Denmark; Crumlin-Pedersen & Olsen 2002), *Mary Rose* (UK; Marsden 2003), the Bremen Cog (Germany; Hoffmann 2011) and *Vasa* (Sweden; Cederlund & Hocker 2006). These sites have captured the public's imagination about underwater archaeology and provided them with the opportunity to see and learn about the maritime history of Europe.

Nevertheless, these examples form only a small fraction of known underwater archaeological sites. As stated in Chapter 2, there are almost 20,000 known monuments under water in the Baltic Sea region alone – 9,000 of which are protected by law. As a result of the huge number of sites known and still being discovered due to offshore and sub-sea development, the past 20 years has seen a move away from raising, conserving and exhibiting underwater shipwreck sites. This is primarily due to financial costs that make such processes non-viable. Instead, there has been an increasing tendency to leave and, where possible, protect sites where they lie on the seabed – so called *in-situ* preservation. This tendency has been politically galvanised in Europe with the *1992 Treaty of Valetta* and internationally with the *2001 UNESCO Convention for the Protection of the Underwater Cultural Heritage* (http://unesdoc.unesco.org/images/0012/001260/126065e.pdf), which came into force on 2 January, 2009. Paragraphs 5 and 10 of *Article 2 – Objectives and General Principles* state that as a first option the underwater cultural heritage should be protected *in situ* and, where possible, non-intrusive methods to document and study these sites *in situ* should be used.

However, to ensure successful *in-situ* protection, an understanding of the threats to underwater sites is required in order to take steps to mitigate against them. Both cultural and natural processes of deterioration can affect underwater sites and have been discussed in Chapter 6. Cultural processes include treasure and souvenir hunting or commercial fishing, whereas the natural processes include physical (sediment erosion), chemical (corrosion) and biological deterioration. **WreckProtect** is primarily concerned with the biological threats to underwater cultural heritage sites consisting of wood and more specifically the threat of wood-boring organisms to sites in the Baltic Sea. The Baltic Sea has traditionally been seen to offer excellent protection to wooden underwater cultural heritage due to its low saline (brackish) waters inhibiting the growth of shipworm – the major cause of biological deterioration. However, in the past 20 years there have been increasing reports of their spread into the Baltic. Understanding the reasons for this spread was one of the main reasons for the **WreckProtect** project and is dealt with in Chapters 7 & 8. Knowledge of the potential spread of shipworm into the Baltic is invaluable for authorities managing the underwater cultural heritage resource in the Baltic. Knowing the geographical areas of their likely occurrence will enable resources to be focused on those sites which are under threat of attack. Knowing your enemy is a pre-requisite to defeating it. However, just knowing where your enemy is will not necessarily defeat it; this is the aim of the current chapter. Shipwrecks can and are being protected from the effects of cultural deterioration by the implementation of legislation, as will be discussed. Unfortunately we cannot legislate against shipworm and there is a need to prevent their attack on shipwrecks. Having assessed and concluded that an archaeologically significant site is potentially at threat from shipworm, are there ways and means of preventing it from attacking a site?

9.2 What will we protect against?

A holistic overview of the deterioration of wooden shipwrecks is required in order to understand how best to preserve them. Thus, a pre-requisite for *in-situ* preservation of shipwrecks is to understand the environment in which the wreck lies and what threats the environment poses to its future preservation – "It is necessary to know your enemy in order to defeat them". In this manner, it may be possible to mitigate against these threats.

It is necessary to understand the nature of the materials present on the site in terms of their state of preservation and what factors can lead to their further deterioration. **Fig. 9.1** shows an idealised view of a wooden shipwreck as it may appear after the wrecking process. Effectively the wreck and its component parts will be exposed to two very differing environments – the open seawater and the sediments of the seabed.

In the open seawater, physical processes, namely sediment erosion ("scour") and biological processes are the major causes of deterioration of wooden and organic materials. Quinn (2006) has summarised the role of scour in the formation of a wreck site which, when in conjunction with wood-boring organisms, can lead to the relatively rapid deterioration of those upper parts of a wreck that are not covered by sediment during the initial wrecking phase. Shipworm or gribble requires dissolved oxygen

Fig. 9.1. An idealised shipwreck on the seabed showing those parts that are exposed to the open seawater and those parts that are buried in the seabed. These two different environments will affect the deterioration processes acting upon the wood (drawing: D. Gregory).

Open Seawater
• *Physical*
Scour due to effects of currents

• *Chemical*
Corrosion of metals

• *Biological*
Activity of wood borers & microorganisms

Seabed
• *Chemical*
Corrosion of metals

• *Biological*
Microbiological decay or organic materials
Microbially induced corrosion of metals

from the surrounding seawater in order to respire and in this respect this is the "limiting factor" for their presence on wreck sites. However, salinity and temperature are also key factors that affect their survival, rate of reproduction and rate of activity (see Chapter 6). Where these parameters are not met, such as is currently apparent in the eastern Baltic, where the salinity is too low for these organisms, wooden wrecks survive intact for centuries but will nevertheless be deteriorated by fungi and bacteria.

However, should the wreck come to be covered by sediment, as a result of sediment accretion rather than erosion, or through the process of liquefaction, such as in the case of the wreck of *Amsterdam* (Marsden 1985), the processes of wood deterioration are predominantly microbiological. Wood will not be degraded by wood borers due to the limited supply of dissolved oxygen within sediments (Gregory 1999) thus preventing their respiration (Turner & Johnson 1971; Becker 1971). Instead deterioration of wood will be biologically mediated though the action of microorganisms, mainly bacteria, which can survive in the anoxic conditions typically found within marine sediments (see Chapter 6).

In order to consider effective methods for protecting sites *in situ* we need to understand what environment the wreck is lying in and identify the threats.

9.3 Methods for the protection of wrecks

If an initial assessment of a site's environment reveals that there are natural threats, or that the site is unstable, strategies should be implemented to mitigate these threats. It is at this stage that an overall evaluation of whether it is feasible, both practically and economically, to leave the site *in situ* should be made. It is argued that *in-situ* preservation is not a panacea for managing the submerged cultural resources but just one of many options. Depending upon the nature of the environment and the historical and archaeological significance of a site, excavation followed either by conservation or re-deposition in a more benign environment, may be the only responsible option to ensure that the wooden archaeological material is preserved.

The wood must be protected against the physical and biological threats. For wooden wrecks exposed to the water column, the most significant threat is wood-boring organisms. For timbers covered with sediment, removal of this layer is the greatest threat. According to the physical and biological degradation processes taking place in the sea and sediments, only physical protection actions are able to stop or decrease these processes. Thus, sites are often covered over using different methods. In the right circumstances, this can both alleviate scour and prevent the activity of wood-boring organisms. Generally, the covering of wooden wreck sites falls into two categories, known as covering methods and barrier methods. These will be discussed and practical tips for their use given below.

Covering methods involve covering timbers with sediment. Barrier methods involve wrapping materials directly around the timbers themselves. Both of these methods aim to create an anoxic environment in which the shipworm cannot survive. In other cases, where the local environment is not conducive to the application of these methods, a site can be excavated and the wooden material re-deposited/reburied in a more benign environment under water or on land. Methods which have, and could be used, for the protection of sites will be discussed below with some tips for their use.

9.4 Evaluation of methods

9.4.1 Covering methods

Covering sites with sediment or other materials functions by limiting the access of oxygen to shipworms. In environments where sediment transport is not prevalent, a covering of just a few centimetres is sufficient to prevent the diffusion of oxygen and thus the growth of shipworm. However, as the shipworm is able to survive and grow as long as its entrance hole is above sediment, the destruction of the wood might take place a couple of decimetres below sediment/water interface. Therefore a recommendation could be to increase the protection layer as much as possible and in this way also the microbial degradation will decrease.

Fig. 9.2. An example of sandbagging: the Bigovica Bay wreck, Montenegro (courtesy of Athena Trakadas, Montenegrin Maritime Archaeology Research Project).

Sand bags

Sand-bagging has often been used in the past as the unit costs are low and they effectively act as a barrier against shipworm by creating an anoxic environment in which the shipworm larvae cannot settle (**Fig. 9.2**).

Tips for use
• Deployment is often expensive and time consuming in terms of person hours used and the difficulty of moving sand bags under water.
• Quite often sand bags are overfilled so that they create an obstruction on the seabed which, if currents are present on the site, can cause scour around the edges of the sand-bagged areas. This undermines them and exposes new areas of the wreck to exposure. As a rule of thumb only fill a sand bag a third to half full. Try to use fine-grained sand with a low organic content. It is then possible to "mould" the sand bags around structures and keep as low a profile as possible.
• It is extremely important that synthetic sand bags are used as any made of natural material will be microbially degraded very rapidly, probably within months.
• Sand bags have been used in many instances. Although as with many of the methods researched there is a lack of systematic assessment or long-term monitoring of the efficacy of *in-situ* stabilisation methods, it may be seen as a temporary method to stabilise. Sand-bagging is effective for small areas and those places where currents threaten to remove archaeological material totally.

Geotextiles

Geotextiles are finely woven or non-woven synthetic fabrics and have been used in coastal engineering to prevent coastal erosion (**Figs. 9.3-9.4**). They are commonly used in marine archaeology to cover areas or

Fig. 9.3. Geotextiles being set over the Zakynthos wreck, Greece (courtesy of Anastasia Pournou).

Fig. 9.4. Timbers of the Zakynthos wreck covered with geotextiles (courtesy of Anastasia Pournou).

trenches at the end of an excavation season. Laying a geotextile over an area and then backfilling enables the cultural layers which have been excavated to be relatively easily re-located come the following season. They have also been used as physical barriers to protect against shipworm on archaeological sites. This will not protect against the microbial degradation. Research carried out on the site known as the Zakynthos wreck in Greece (Pournou et al. 2001) has shown that a specific grade of geotextile, Terram 4000 (www.terram.com), was effective at preventing the larvae of shipworm settling on the wood. Similarly in the EU *MoSS* project, work with geotextiles showed the same results, as has research on the wrecks of *HMS Colossus* (Camidge 2009) and the Swash Channel wreck (Palma 2009). The flexibility of the fabrics makes them ideal to mould around timbers which are standing proud of the seabed.

Tips for use
• Geotextiles such as Terram and Propex (www.geotextile.com) can be extremely buoyant, and as a standard roll is 4 m wide, it is good idea to wrap the geotextile around a metal rod in order to add weight. Lengths of up to 10 m can easily be deployed in this manner.
• If large areas are to be covered, insert eyelets in the geotextile, which can then be joined using cable ties in order to cover a larger area.
• When unrolling, it is often easier if there are two divers for this task.
• Ensure that any current is behind the divers, which will also facilitate unrolling of the geotextile.
• A following diver can place sand bags to weight the geotextile as it is being rolled out in order to prevent it from floating away.

Covering with the help of sediment transport

Although these guidelines are to protect sites from the threat of wood borers, in particular *Teredo navalis*, underwater archaeological sites are also threatened by sediment transport. There are several methods that could be used in which sediment transport is used to an advantage. They work on the principle that if there is sediment transport in the waters around the site this can be trapped and held in position in order to cover the site.

Artificial sea grass

A method which is used in the offshore industry for stabilising submerged pipelines and cables involves the use of artificial sea grass. There are several proprietary makes on the market, all of which function on the same principle. One of the major suppliers of artificial sea grasses is Seabed Scour Control Systems (http://www.sscsystems.com). The way the system works is graphically described below (**Figs. 9.5-9.6**).

Fig. 9.5. Artificial sea grass, unrolled (photo: Peter Moe Astrup).

Tips for use
• Ensure that there is sediment transport on the site. Look for bed forms, i.e sand ripples on the seabed.

• Where possible, align the long edge of the net perpendicular to the direction of any current in order to trap the maximum amount of sediment.

• Make sure that if there is any current when positioning the mats that it is behind the diver in order to facilitate the rolling out of the net.

• After installing sea grass, it is beneficial to "rustle" the fronds regularly to make sure they are not filled with seaweed or other detritus.

Fig. 9.6. Artificial sea grass, rolled (photo: David Gregory).

• The mats can be quite expensive, especially in the scheme of archaeological projects. The artificial sea grass from Seabed Scour controls are supplied as 5 x 3 m rolls.

• Relatively easy to deploy from smaller vessels. However, these mats are fastened by anchors which penetrate 50 cm into the seabed and could damage underlying archaeology.

• In strong currents the sea grass fronds can actually lie down flat and are ineffectual at collecting sediment, however, they do deflect currents. Collected sediment can be scoured out.

Notable examples where artificial sea grasses have been used or trialled are on the wrecks of *William Salthouse* (Steyne 2009), *James Matthews* (Richards et al. 2009) and the Hårbølle wreck (Gregory et al. 2008).

Debris netting/Shade cloth

Fig. 9.7. Schematic of how the debris netting functions (drawing: M. Manders).

Debris netting is the net-like material which is used when carrying out construction work on buildings in order to prevent any building debris from falling on passersby. It was first developed for archaeological use in the Netherlands and was further developed in the EU *MoSS Project* (Manders 2004). The debris netting functions in a similar way to artificial sea grass. The idea is that the net is fastened loosely over the structure to be protected, so that it floats in the water. As with the artificial sea grass the method is dependent upon there being currents and sediment transport in the water. If there is sediment transport and the sediment is of a fine enough grain size to pass through the mesh, then, because of friction, the sediments will be slowed, come out of suspension, and become trapped under the net creating a burial mound under water (**Fig. 9.7**).

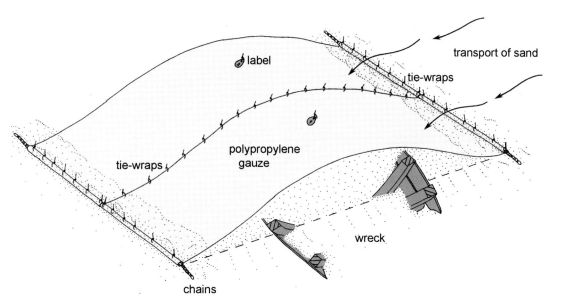

Tips for use (Figs. 9.8-9.9):
• Ensure that there is sediment transport on the site and that you have an idea of what kinds of sediment are being transported in terms of particle size.
• Select debris netting which has a mesh size large enough for the sediment being transported to pass through. A good type of net where there is a compromise between strength and mesh size is what is termed a "Windbreak net" 230 gm^{-2} mesh size 5 x 2 mm.
• Most debris nets are supplied in 50 m rolls which are 2-3 m in width. Cut the length desired and wrap the net around a metal rod to give weight as the net is extremely buoyant.

Fig. 9.8. A) A prepared net being carried to the site. B) Fixing the leading edge of the net with metal hooks. C) Rolling out the net over the site. D) Fixing fishing buoys to the net for extra buoyancy (photos: Jørgen Dencker).

• Insert eyelets on the edges of the net both to enable fixing of the net into the seabed and joining nets together.

• When joining nets together, make sure there is an overlap between the two. In this way you avoid getting holes between the nets when they tighten due to the sediment build up.

• Where possible, align the long edge of the net perpendicular to the direction of any current in order to trap the maximum amount of sediment.

• Make sure that any current is coming from behind the diver when positioning the net in order to facilitate its rolling out and also to avoid entanglement.

• The net must not be stretched tight on the seabed but should be loose. For example, when trying to cover a length of 5 m, a 6 m-long length of net is cut and only rolled out to 5 m so that there is enough loose material to float in the water column.

• The net can be fixed to the seabed either with long pegs that penetrate the seabed or heavy material such as anchor chains or sand bags.

• In order to give the net buoyancy, attach small fishing buoys to raise the net from the seabed.

• After initial installation, monitor the net and shake it to remove any sediment that is lying on top of the net and attach further buoys, if necessary.

• Ensure the net is not tearing where pins have been used to anchor it.

• Parts of the wreck that protrude from the seabed may initially damage the nets that are loosely placed on the site. To avoid this, one can cover these parts with sand bags or add sediment with a water dredge before or just after installing the nets.

Fig. 9.9. A completed net installation waiting to catch sediment (photo: David Gregory).

The method has been used successfully on several sites notably the wreck of the Burgzand Noord 10 in the Netherlands (Manders 2004; 2006b), *Avondster* in Sri Lanka (Manders 2006a) and the Darsser Cog in Germany (Jöns 2003) and was successfully trialled around the wreck of the Hårbølle site in Denmark (Gregory 2008). However, trials of the netting on *HMS Colossus* (Camidge 2009) and the Swash Channel wreck (Palma 2009) were not deemed successful. This again stresses the need to understand the way *in-situ* stabilisation methods work and that they are not necessarily effective on every type of site.

Debris net producers:
UK: Coastal nets: http://www.coastalnets.co.uk/industrial_main.htm
USA: Several: http://www.macraesbluebook.com/search/product_company_list.cfm?prod_code=5182050
South Korea: Tasco Ltd: http://www.alibaba.com/product-free/102525712/Scaffolding_Net.html

Covering with sediment

Reburial under water

As discussed, shipworm cannot survive for long periods in the absence of dissolved oxygen and it is the fact that wood, when buried in the seabed, will only be susceptible to slow microbial degradation caused by fungi and bacteria due to the lack of oxygen in marine sediments. Thus, covering or re-burying wood is one way of preventing further attack by shipworm. Covering or re-burial has been achieved by several methods, including natural or intentional backfilling of timbers after excavation, sediment dumping or deflection of sediments to cover a site *in situ*. Furthermore, artefacts have been re-buried after raising and documenting. These methods and where they have been used, will be discussed.

Backfilling

It is rare that a shipwreck site will be completely excavated during the course of a single excavation period. Alternately a site may not be completely excavated if the whole hull is not to be removed. Thus, between excavation periods sites are often either purposely re-covered with sediment or left to be covered naturally by sediment. This covering is essential if the area is known to be affected by shipworm. The summer months, when most excavations take place, are prime breeding time for shipworms, thus it is extremely important that sites are not left uncovered. However, for backfilling to be successful it should be established beforehand that the sediments will not be removed due to sediment transport.

Sediment drop

Backfilling is usually carried out by divers on the seabed using suction dredges or buckets and spades, simply to fill in the trenches created during excavation. However, this can also be carried out in combination with a sediment drop. As the name suggests, sediments in a boat or barge are dropped over the site and they are either left to naturally settle on the site or are moved by divers to backfill any exposed trenches. This approach has been used on many sites as it is seen to be cost effective as divers do not have to be used so much, and that large areas can be covered at one time. However, as with all these methods one has to understand the environment in which the methods are being carried out. For example, if there are currents in the water, sediment may not reach the site. Furthermore, if the sediment is not covered with a geotextile, sand bags, geo-membrane or other form of barrier sediment, it can be lost due to subsequent sediment transport. Even though a relatively thin coating of sediment is enough to prevent the action of shipworm the depth of sediment cover needs also to be deep enough to reduce the effects of microbial deterioration.

Reburial

One of the first attempts of controlled reburial of archaeological remains under water was carried out in the 1980s. From 1980 to 1984, Parks Canada excavated the remains of the Basque whaler *San Juan* in Red Bay, Labrador. Following the excavation, raising and documentation of the wreck, the timbers were reburied to protect them against biological, chemical and especially physical deterioration due to ice flows. What set this early project aside from other reburial attempts at the time was that monitoring of the reburied timbers and the surrounding reburial environment was planned from the outset – as will be discussed in the next section. Sand bags and the ballast from the ship were used to construct an underwater cofferdam where the timbers were placed in several layers, each separated by a layer of sand. Modern wood blocks were placed alongside each layer for subsequent removal and analysis. The burial mound was then covered with a heavy-duty plastic tarpaulin anchored by concrete-filled rubber tyres.

A similar project was recently started in Sweden, which set out to validate the efficacy of reburial of archaeological materials in the marine environment. The 'Reburial and Analysis of Archaeological Remains' project focuses on the reburial of artefacts from the wreck of *Fredericus* (1719) in the Swedish island port of Marstrand. Archaeological investigations were initiated in the harbour because of the need to reinforce the quay.

Two major investigations were undertaken. One was an excavation of the wreck of the frigate *Fredericus*, sunk in a battle between Sweden and Denmark, and the other was an investigation of an area alongside the quay, which revealed cultural remains dating back to the 17th century. These two excavations yielded approximately 10,000 artefacts. Full conservation treatment of all excavated artefacts was considered both impractical and unnecessary from an archaeological perspective and it was decided that 85-90% of the finds should be re-buried after proper archaeological documentation.

Amongst other materials (a shipwreck rarely consists of just wood), modern wood samples were left exposed to seawater and reburied at various depths down to 50 cm. Preliminary results after three years of reburial show that those samples left exposed to seawater were rapidly and heavily degraded by wood borers, whereas those covered by sediments were microbially degraded. The results reflect the results of the Red Bay wreck and other experiments on re-burial of wood – that even a thin covering of sediments is significant enough to limit the amount of oxygen in the sediment for shipworm to survive.

Tips for use

• Assess whether there is sediment transport over a site. If there is and it is significant, one of the previously described methods may need to be applied or the reburied site covered with a geotextile, plastic geomembrane or coarser grained material (gravel) to ensure the sediment is not removed.
• Local sediment from surrounding areas is often used for reburial and should be characterised for its suitability. It is recommended that the porosity and organic content of any sediment should at least be assessed. Sediment should ideally be fine grained sands, which are less porous and naturally contain less organic material due to their larger particle size. This leads to lower rates of mineralisation when the dominant process is sulphate reduction, which is typical of marine sediments. This contrasts with the higher rates of mineralisation in more porous finer grained sediment with higher organic contents.
• An optimal depth of burial is dependent upon the nature of the sediment to be used. However, even a thin covering of sediment will limit the oxygen content sufficiently to prevent the survival of wood borers.
• Try to re-bury artefacts in one layer so that it is easier to return to the area and remove timbers which may be required for further analysis.
• Ensure that there is a good site plan for any reburial and that it is (relatively) easy to come back and find specific timbers.
• Ensure that any materials used in the reburial, including labels, containers, etc., are durable.

9.4.2 Barrier methods

Geotextiles have already been discussed and they can serve as a barrier method. Other materials include plastic films such as PVC barrier materials. Flexible barrier materials which have been placed around pilings may also have potential applications for archaeological timbers which are standing too far proud of the seabed to cover with sediment. These, to the best of the authors' knowledge, have not been used archaeologically. However, they would function by creating a physical and oxygen free barrier around the timber to be protected. In this manner the shipworm larvae cannot attach themselves to the wood surface. Furthermore, any living shipworm in the timber will not be able to respire due to the lack of oxygen. There are several proprietary manufacturers of these materials. One of the major manufacturers is Pile-gard (http://www.barrierimp.com/) and the flexibility of the material would appear to allow the material to be moulded around timbers.

9.5 Follow up: monitoring as part of management

Protection methods cannot guarantee equal protection under all conditions. It is therefore important to monitor protected sites and thus to manage any change. *In-situ* preservation should not stop once the site has been stabilised. Monitoring of stabilised sites is necessary to ensure continued stability. Furthermore, although a newly discovered site may be relatively stable and thus not immediately require any active mitigation strategies, environmental and/or physical changes may occur which require additional mitigation strategies at a later date. In this context, monitoring is essential. As discussed, shipwrecks exist in a dynamic equilibrium with their environments and subsequent changes may occur through storm events or impacts of a cultural nature. This is equally valid for sites where active mitigation strategies, such as reburial, have been implemented. Monitoring means keeping track of the condition of a site and its protection methods and registering all changes.

Therefore, monitoring should be compared with baseline data. The most ideal procedure would be to have data prior to undertaking physical *in-situ* protection. After installation the same data are collected and a time-line for further monitoring developed. This time line is an indication of how often a site needs to be monitored in the future. However, this can change over time for a number of reasons. For example, new information might indicate that severe changes are currently occurring or will in the near future and the site has to be examined more often.

As with the various processes of deterioration, monitoring should consider the two broadly different environments of open seawater/seabed and within the seabed. Within the open seawater we are concerned with physical and biological processes of deterioration namely sediment transport (erosion/accretion) and the activity of wood-boring organisms mainly, secondly the microbial degradation. Furthermore, the condition of timbers should be assessed to ensure that they are not further degrading.

Open water and the surface of the seabed

Data for monitoring open water can be acquired in the following ways:
1) Technical devices such as data loggers
2) By obtaining this information from large (oceanographic) institutes that are measuring the data for other purposes
3) Another way to measure the water column is to place sacrificial objects in the water and measure their deterioration rate over time
4) Taking water samples and post-recovery analyses

The seabed can be measured in a few ways:
1) Visually, by divers
2) With marine geophysics such as single beam, multibeam, side scan sonar
3) Traditional sounding (sounding lead)
4) Laser, aerial photography and satellite

The visual inspection of a site can be achieved by sending down divers or by using camera mounted Remote Operating Vehicles (ROVs). Visual inspection can tell us something about the pure physical conditions of a site and if, e.g. parts of the wreck are being exposed. Also, divers can identify if a site is being attacked by *Teredo navalis*.

Marine Geophysics

Many governmental institutions now have access to marine geophysical methods, such as multibeam echo sounder (MBES) which can be used to monitor the net effects of sediment transport over a wreck site. Repeated surveys carried out at different times using MBES can be digitally subtracted from each other in order to map where there are areas of net accretion and net scour of sediment (**Fig. 9.10**). Although this shows formation products rather than processes, in terms of *in-situ* preservation it provides a reproducible method to quantify changes over an entire site.

Although not recording actual depth, side-scan sonar can also be used to monitor the changes on protected submerged archaeological sites and their environment. This equipment, which can scan large areas of the sea-

Fig. 9.10. *Digitally subtracting multibeam recordings from different years to analyse net accretion or scour (MACHU Project).*

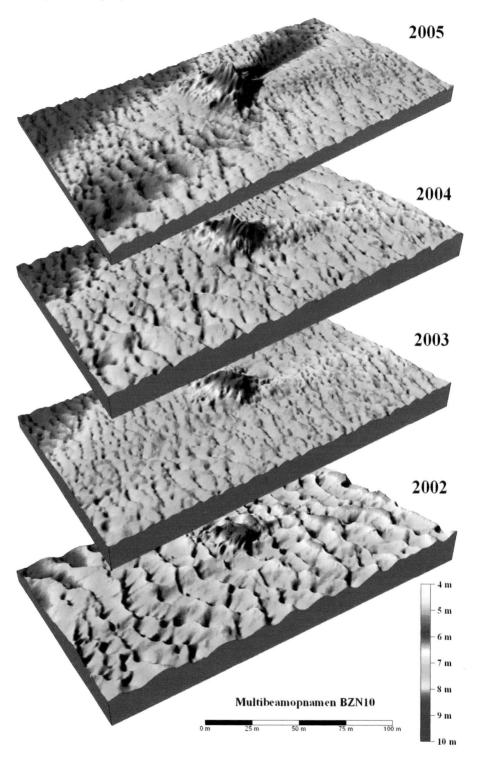

2005

2004

2003

2002

Multibeamopnamen BZN10

0 m   25 m   50 m   75 m   100 m

4 m
5 m
6 m
7 m
8 m
9 m
10 m

bed in a relatively short time, has become very cheap in the last couple of years and its use is now widespread. In order to study on-going sedimentary processes, current profilers and sediment sampling (through coring or using sediment traps) can be placed on sites in order to model the likelihood of sediment transport. The presence of actual suspended particulate matter in the water column can also be monitored using turbidity sensors/loggers. This is a relatively simple method of ascertaining if there is sediment transport and in particular when considering the use of artificial sea grass or netting materials to stabilise a site.

Presence or absence of wood borers

In terms of monitoring the presence and activity of wood-boring organisms over a site it is not always easy to monitor their activity directly on exposed timbers. However, this can be monitored by the placement of sacrificial blocks of modern wood around a site and recording organisms' presence or absence. If they are present it is highly likely that any newly exposed timbers will also be colonised and thus steps to mitigate their effects can be taken. As can be seen from Chapter 6, the temperature, dissolved oxygen and salinity of the water will also have an effect on the growth of wood boring organisms. These parameters can similarly be logged using data loggers but it is now often possible to obtain such data from Governmental institutions that are monitoring water quality parameters.

Within the seabed

Nearly all biogeochemical processes in young sediments are directly or indirectly connected with the degradation of organic matter (Rullkötter 2000). The decomposition of organic matter by organisms involves oxidation – reduction (Redox) reactions (Schulz 2000). These reactions follow a well-documented succession with various chemical species or electron acceptors being utilised based on the amount of energy they yield (Froelich et al. 1979).

In marine sediments, the sequence of electron acceptor utilisation can be observed spatially in horizontal layers of increasing depth. In typical coastal marine sediment, only the first few millimetres of the sediment are oxygenated, though bioturbation by invertebrates and advection may extend this oxygenated zone downwards. For a few centimetres under the oxygenated zone, nitrate serves as the electron acceptor followed by manganese and iron oxides. Below this, sulphate is the principal electron acceptor and sulphate reduction is often the dominant process in shallow marine sediments due to the high concentrations of sulphate in seawater.

Methanogenesis is usually confined to the sulphate-depleted deeper sediment layers, though the generated methane may diffuse upward into the zone of sulphate reduction. Thus, the deterioration of organic matter still occurs in anoxic environments due to the activity of anaerobic organisms, albeit at a slower rate.

In terms of monitoring within sediments, the dissolved oxygen content, concentrations of various chemical species, porosity and organic content of the sediment can all yield information about some of the ongoing biogeochemical processes in the sediment and indicate the rate of deterioration of organic matter. A monitoring programme can use data logging devices or analysis of pore water taken from core samples. Summing up, the following parameters should be assessed in order to get an idea of the nature of the buried environment:

• Dissolved oxygen content
• Redox potential
• Sulphate/Sulphide and also total sulphur content
• Organic content of sediment
• Porosity of sediment

The aforementioned parameters will give a good indication of whether the environment is oxic or anoxic (with or without oxygen) and which dominant process are taking place in the sediment.

In order to check what is happening to wooden materials, small sacrificial samples of wood can be included as part of a monitoring programme as the rate and cause of deterioration can be assessed microscopically in order to confirm biogeochemical monitoring of sediments. For monitoring of physical *in-situ* protection within the seabed, one can consider subbottom profiling (Manders 2009b; Plets et al. 2009). This technique has been in use for monitoring wreck sites that have been protected with debris netting.

Condition of timbers

It is important to get an overview of the actual state of preservation of the wood when considering its *in-situ* preservation. Simply put, is the wood in a stable enough state to be left where it is? Are there threats of further deterioration if the wood is left *in situ*? What effects will any proposed mitigation strategies have on the wood?

In terms of assessing the effects of wood-boring organisms, a simple thin metal probe can be used and simply pressed into the wood. Often, if shipworms are present, or have previously been active in the wood, there is little or no resistance. This is unfortunately only a qualitative assessment but will give an indication of the presence of shipworms. Alternately, a more elaborate, yet similar method to the metal probe, can be used, known as the Pilodyn. The Pilodyn was originally developed to assess the extent of soft-rot decay in telegraph poles in service. The Pilodyn works by firing a spring-loaded blunt pin into the wood, to a maximum depth of 40 mm. The depth of penetration of the pin is indicated on a scale on the side of the instrument. The more degraded the wood, the further the pin will penetrate. In the hands of an experienced diver, it is a relatively cheap, simple and robust tool for non-destructively mapping the state of preservation of timbers on the seabed. In order to assess the overall state of preservation of the wood that remains, density is a good parameter. As discussed, microorganisms operate on a cellular level and, as they remove cell wall material this is replaced by water. As a result, the more degraded the wood is, the lower the density of the wood. Density can be assessed using cores taken *in situ* with an increment borer which are subsequently processed in the laboratory. The most accurate method for examination of the condition of the timber is microscopic analyses of core samples, which will reveal state and degree of degradation and the actual cause of degradation.

Under water data logger suppliers
http://www.ysi.com/applicationsdetail.php?Ocean-and-Coastal-Monitoring

9.6 Guidelines for the protection of wrecks

WreckProtect guidelines

The protection methods for *in-situ* preservation described in this chapter have also been developed by the **WreckProtect** consortium into guidelines with hands-on tools for the management and protection of the underwater cultural heritage. Although the guidelines have a special focus on the Baltic, they can be of use and applied anywhere else in the world.

   The guidelines are a complement and alternative document to this book and prepared in such a way that they contain all the information needed for a specific job. This means that the guidelines for the protection of wooden submerged cultural heritage contains a list of methods that can be used to protect physically the sites, but also information on why sites should be (physically) protected and what to do before and after the sites have been protected *in situ*.

   Short chapters include a summary of important information and a list of suggested reading for more detailed information.

   PDF versions of the two guidelines can be found on the website (*www.wreckprotect.eu*).

9.7 Costs for *in-situ* preservation versus full conservation
Charlotte Gjelstrup Björdal

Since very few shipwrecks in the world have been protected *in situ*, or excavated, raised, conserved and exhibited to the public, it is difficult to give the true costs for these actions. Another problem is a lack of information as these costs are not fully clarified or explained in the literature. The investigation done by **WreckProtect** to elucidate the costs and the difference between these two actions is therefore based on both personal communication and available literature. The reader will soon realise that despite small errors and limited information, there is a great difference in costs between these two actions. It is the intention of this chapter to give stakeholders and managers' insight into the costs associated with both alternatives, so that decisions of future management of important wrecks can be based on realistic updated costs.

Costs for conservation (including raising and display)

There are only a few shipwrecks in the world that have been excavated from a marine environment and subsequently conserved and displayed. The warship *Vasa* in Sweden is probably the most well-known example, followed by other Northern European wrecks such as *Mary Rose* (UK) and the Bremen cog (D). The modest number of shipwrecks exhibited to the public today is strictly related to the enormous costs for these actions. No costs are given in the literature for the raising and treatment of *Vasa*. The decision to raise the ship in 1961 was not controlled by economic matters *per se*, but rather driven by enthusiasm. This is different from the way of decision-making nowadays, where we want to know all the implications beforehand.

The investigation by **WreckProtect** to elucidate the costs for full excavation, conservation and display of shipwrecks, shows in most cases that the complete costs were not possible to obtain. However, information from six different case studies gives a good picture of the costs that could be incurred at the different stages in the process – from excavation to display. Generally, larger wrecks have larger costs, and a wreck intended for storage is a little less expensive than a wreck intended for display. Cheapest is a small-size wreck, the 11 m-long Göta wreck, found on land in Sweden, which in total had a cost of €1.9 mil. (pers. comm., S. Wranne, SVK, Sweden).

The costs related to *Mary Rose*, which today is receiving a full conservation treatment for display in Portsmouth, UK, gives us the most transparent and best information regarding the full cost for a large shipwreck.

Known and estimated costs related to **Mary Rose**

At the ARC-Nautica Conference in Dubrovnic, Croatia, 2009, marine archaeologist Christopher Dobbs from The Mary Rose Trust gave an account of the total costs related to *Mary Rose*. He was able to divide the costs into the following categories: £2.8 mil. for the raising; £6.1 mil. for management and conservation of hull and objects 1982-2009; and £4.2 mil. for further PEG impregnation of the hull (estimation for 2009-2012). Much of the work for the underwater excavation was done on a voluntary basis, and was not included (Dobbs 2007). This work took 23,000 hours in active diving time (pers. comm., C. Dobbs). The future costs for an adequate building for display and finishing the final phase of conservation (air-drying) is planned and estimated to cost around £35 mil. If we summarise the previous costs, including a new museum building, the total sum is approximately **£48 mil.** or **€59 mil.** (2011 rate).

In addition, if the diving was carried out today by professional divers, the hours spent would probably be less, but the price would be much higher. If 15,000 hours were required, the costs could roughly be estimated at £5 mil., which should be added to the total sum.

Costs for *in-situ* preservation

For protection of a wreck *in situ*, there are some parameters that always will affect the total expenses more than others. These are primarily related to the site and the environment surrounding the wreck, and secondly to the hull itself. The factors that will have the highest impact on the costs are identified below:

• Environment (currents, visibility, etc.)
• Depth (work-related difficulties increase with increased depth)
• Size of the wreck above seabed (vertical and horizontal dimensions)
• Size of the site that should be included in the protection area

Another type of parameter affecting the costs is related to the country in question. Salaries, costs of ship rental, and also work-related policies and legal frameworks vary within Europe. The costs for materials used are usually relatively small. It is evident that the personnel costs for professional divers and maritime archaeologists are the main expenses, followed by costs for rental of diving vessels and equipment necessary for diving.

For *Stora Sofia* (Sweden), *Hårböllebro* (Denmark), *Burgzand* (the Netherlands), and the *Zakyntos* (Greece), the approximate total costs varied between €46,000 and €71,000. The larger ships had the highest costs, and it took up to 10 working days to complete the job despite the method applied.

Conclusions

In-situ protection techniques provide stakeholders with a useful and cheaper alternative for protection and preservation of important cultural heritage. *Mary Rose,* which is of the same size as *Stora Sofia*, will cost about €53 mil. to conserve and display, whereas the *in-situ* protection of *Stora Sofia* cost around €70,000. A simple and rough calculation tells us that around 700 historical ships could be preserved *in situ* for future generations for the costs of <u>one</u> wreck conserved and displayed. However, the costs do not stop here, as the *in-situ* preservation requires future long-term monitoring, and wrecks on display require continuous control and care.

As there recently has been discussion on raising the "Ghost Ship" found near Gotland, in international waters (see Chapter 2.2.3), these figures could have great importance in the discussion of strategies for management of such finds. It is very clear that the costs related to the marine archaeological underwater excavations are extremely high as they involve divers with specialised underwater equipment, ships with all relevant technical instruments, as well as a high operational safety level.

When the question of costs is raised to stakeholders of the Vasa Museum, the answer is that it has been paid off. *Vasa* is today the number one tourist attraction in Stockholm, and is of great economic importance for the city and the museum itself. But for other "less attractive" shipwrecks, the situation may not be that positive. The fact is that the daily costs for storage, maintenance and display might endanger the economy of a smaller museum.

We have to be aware that not all negative and positive effects can be as easily taken into account when deciding whether to excavate, conserve and display material from a site. Indirect positive effects may be, for example, also the creation of awareness, identity building and capacity building in underwater cultural heritage, underwater archaeology and conservation. The raising of *Mary Rose* in 1982 was witnessed by over 60 million people world-wide on live television. Then there is the economic effect of countries and cities becoming known by the general public and thus triggering tourist traffic. All these have a long-term effect and cannot always easily be pinpointed and related to what has been invested to the excavation, raising and conservation of a wreck from a specific site.

10. Future research
Charlotte Gjelstrup Björdal, David Gregory & Martijn Manders

Managers of cultural heritage need efficient methods to preserve the underwater cultural heritage. The cost to raise, conserve and display cultural remains is very large and there need to be good reasons to do so. Long term *in-situ* preservation is therefore an important part of underwater cultural heritage management. The *2001 UNESCO Convention on the Protection of the Submerged Cultural Heritage* – amongst others – therefore mentions it as the first option to consider. By developing and applying efficient methods, valuable sites can be protected and saved for future generations.

The question might be asked, "Why should we save these historic shipwrecks and other underwater archaeological sites"? Other than just to display the majesty of elegant old ships for future generations to enjoy, each wreck site, for example, can hold information on the life people lived in a fixed period of time and, in particular, life on board. They also contain information on building techniques, wood use and even shipbuilding design, trade, exchange, and warfare.

During the **WreckProtect** project it became obvious that knowledge of the complex physical, chemical and biological processes related to the preservation conditions of wrecks in the Baltic is still limited even though more research is being conducted in this area. The same situation appeared when trying to identify adequate methods for the protection of wrecks. Research publications provided us with knowledge to a certain level, but when it came to more detailed information on, for example, ecological levels for survival of *Teredo navalis* in brackish waters, decay rates, changes in wood cell wall chemistry and physical properties, or fungal soft-rot species in the Baltic Sea, data were not easily obtainable.

At the moment there are no effective methods to protect the unique well-preserved shipwreck sites in the eastern and northern parts of the Baltic Sea. Today the threat of *Teredo navalis* in the northern area is very low and, according to the developed GIS model on prediction of decay, the risk for attack will not increase within the next ten years. However, as described, microbial decay is an on-going process everywhere in the Baltic Sea, and also in this area. The effect of fungal and bacterial attack is initially a softening of the wood surface layers and is slowly followed by interior degradation. This results in changes in wood cell wall chemistry in combination with physical underwater forces like currents, sand erosion and waves; the important wood surface layers of shipwrecks, with information on tool marks and decoration, are at risk of disappearing.

Moreover, a shipwreck's construction itself may weaken and the whole structure might collapse within time. For this reason, adequate methods are needed in order to secure the integrity of large-sized wrecks resting on the seabed. As this is an extremely complicated task, development should take place in a cross-disciplinary context.

Methods exist for the protection of smaller-sized shipwrecks or fragments of wrecks, where most of the hull is already protected by sediment and only small elements are visible above the seabed. These methods could be further developed, however, especially in regard to systems that ensure the stability of the physical protective layer (often sediment) that is added to the site. In extreme environments, such as sites with strong currents, sediment erosion, and sediment transport, there is a demand for solid tailor-made solutions.

Shipwrecks can be protected if we take advantage of some of the forces in nature. One method for the protection of wrecks, debris netting, is based on the use of natural sediment transportation (see Chapter 9). Understanding sediment transportation at a wreck site is therefore very important, both for the protection and also uncovering of sites. This is therefore one of the important parameters that should be studied more closely and related to individual sites. This has been extensively done at the EU-Culture 2000 programme Project MACHU (*www.machuproject. eu*).

Usually timbers embedded in sediment degrade extremely slowly. Here, in near anaerobic environments, marine borers and soft-rot fungi are not active and the only degrading organisms are erosion bacteria. It will be necessary to focus our study a bit more on these erosion bacteria in order to learn more about their requirements for growth and reproduction. In this way we may eventually also find a method to stop them from deteriorating submerged archaeological wood. This study could be executed in a laboratory and by field experiments, using the present available knowledge accumulated in previous (EU) projects such as BACPOLES.

What is urgently needed is information on the decay status of historical wrecks in the Baltic Sea today. Well-defined samples from a large number of wrecks over a wide geographical area should be collected in cooperation with marine archaeologists. These wrecks should be examined in order to get a better picture of the decay processes taking place on a long-term scale, and not at least to give stakeholders the status of the shipwreck itself.

WreckProtect has provided cultural heritage with the first tool for tracking *Teredo navalis* in the Baltic Sea. This GIS model is the best available model today, and based on the current state of knowledge. It is very important that the model is continuously tested and refined – certainly the model is at its weakest in coastal areas, where there was limited information available. Field experiments, where sound wood is exposed at various sites in the Baltic in order to determine the presence of *Teredo* *navalis,* would help this process. In addition, laboratory experiments aimed at testing the survival and reproduction of shipworm would provide valuable information for understanding the species' spread.

It was found that currents control the spread of shipworm more than expected. These determine, for a large part, whether *Teredo navalis* can or cannot spread successfully into the Baltic Sea. Information on the directions of underwater currents should be studied and specifically around shipwrecks. In terms of monitoring cost effective and accessibly geophysical monitoring systems should be developed in order to assess an overall site.

By using these methods the "products" of any sediment transport can be assessed – as has been shown on the BZN 10 site in the Netherlands where multibeam was used. In terms of monitoring in sediments although data-logging systems and sensors are available to measure various parameters in the sediment it is still difficult to determine specifically what parameters are relevant to monitor in terms decay rate for wood degrading fungi and bacteria. Future work aiming at dissemination of obtained knowledge to stakeholders and managers of underwater cultural heritage is very important.

Cooperation, curiosity and respect within and in between the different **WreckProtect** disciplines involved could give unique results and a true value for the long-term preservation of cultural heritage.

References and suggested reading

Adams, J., 2003. *Ships, Innovation and Social Change* (Stockholm, University of Stockholm).

Adams, J., Norman, P., & Rönnby, J., 1991. Rapport från marinarkeologisk vrakbesiktning, Franska Stenarna, Nämdöfjärden. *Marinarkeologisk tidskrift* (Stockholm) 2: 8-10.

Adams, J., & Rönnby, J., 1996. *Furstens Fartyg* (Uppsala, Swedish National Maritime Museum).

Adams, J., & Rönnby, J., 1998. *Nämdöfjärdens Kraveln* (Unpublished report, Stockholm County Authority).

Adams, J., & Rönnby, J., 2005. *Nämdöfjärdens Kraveln 2003-4* (Unpublished report, Stockholm County Authority).

Adams, J., & Rönnby, J., 2009. Kraveln – marinarkeologiska undersökningar av ett skeppsvrak från tidig 1500-tal i Nämdöfjärden, Stockholms skärgård. In: K. Schoerner (ed.), *Skärgård och örlog. Nedslag i Stockholms skärgårds tidiga historia* (Stockholm, Kungl. Vitterhets historie och antikvitets akademien): 73-102.

Adams, J. & Rönnby, J., in press. One of his Majesty's 'beste kraffwells'. The wreck of an early carvel-built ship at Franska Stenarna, Sweden. *International Journal of Nautical Archaeology*.

Ahlström, C., 1979. *Sjunkna Skepp* (Lund, Natur och kultur).

Al Hamdani, Z., & Reker, J. (eds.), 2007. Towards Marine Landscapes in the Baltic Sea. *BALANCE Interim Report* 10. *Publication of the Geological Survey of Denmark and Greenland.* (Available online at: http://balance-eu.org/; Accessed November, 2011).

Andrén, T., 2003a. Baltiska Issjön – eller hur det började. *Havsutsikt* 1: 4-5.

Andrén, T., 2003b. Yoldiahavet – en viktig parentes. *Havsutsikt* 2: 6-7.

Andrén, T., 2003c. Ancylussjön – fortfarande ett mysterium. *Havsutsikt* 3: 8-9.

Andrén, T., 2004. Littorinahavet – en salt historia. *Havsutsikt* 1: 8-9.

Anonymous, 2003. *Treasures of the Baltic Sea. A hidden wealth of culture.* Report number 46 (Stockholm, Swedish Maritime Museums).

Anonymous, 2006. *Rutilus: Strategies for a Sustainable Development of the Underwater Cultural Heritage in the Baltic Sea Region.* Report dbr 1267/03-51 (Stockholm, Swedish Maritime Museums).

Appelqvist C., forthcoming. *The geographical distribution of shipworms along the Swedish coast and around the Danish island Bornholm.*

BACC Author Team, 2008. *Assessment of Climate Change for the Baltic Sea Basin* (Berlin, Springer-Verlag).

Bartolini, M., Capretti, C., Galotta, G., Giachi, G., Macchioni, N., Nugari, M.P., & Pizzo, B., 2004. Il porto di Neapolis: indagini diagnostiche. *Archaeologia Maritima Mediterranea* 1: 82-91.

Becker, G., 1971. On the Biology, Physiology and Ecology of Marine Wood Boring Crustaceans. In: E.B. Gareth Jones & S.K. Eltringham (eds.), *Marine Borers, Fungi and Fouling organisms of Wood. Proceedings of the OECD Workshop Organised by the Committee Investigating the Preservation of Wood in the Marine Environment, 27th March-3rd April, 1968* (Paris, Organisation for Economic Co-operation and Development): 304-326.

Beltrame, C., 2002. Investigating Processes of Wreck Formation: Wrecks on the Beach Environment in the Mediterranean Sea. *Archeologia subacquea. Studi, ricerche e documenti* III: 381-398.

Bergstrand, T., & Nyström Godfrey, I. (eds.), 2007. *Reburial and analyses of archaeological remains. Studies on the effect of reburial on archaeological materials performed in Marstrand, Sweden 2002-2005. The RAAR Project.* Kulturhistoriska dokumentationer nr 20 (Uddevalla, Bohusläns Museums förlag).

Bettazzi, F., Giachi, G., Staccioli, G., & Chimichi, S., 2003. Chemical characterisation of wood of Roman ships brought to light in the recently discovered ancient harbour of Pisa (Tuscany, Italy). *Holzforschung* 57.4: 373-376.

Björdal, C., Daniel, G., & Nilsson, T., 2000. Depth of burial, an important factor in controlling bacterial decay of waterlogged archaeological poles. *International Biodeterioration & Biodegradation* 45: 15-26.

Björdal, C.G., & Nilsson, T., 2007. Outline and results from the 'Vasa Wood Project' with emphasis on the microscopic investigations In: K. Strætkvern & H. Huisman (eds.), *Proceedings of the 10th ICOM Group on Wet Organic Archaeological Materials Conference, Amsterdam, 2007* (Amersfoort, Rijksdienst voor Archeologie, Cultuurlandschap en Monumenten): 483-490.

Björdal, C.G., & Nilsson, T., 2008. Reburial of shipwrecks in marine sediments. A long term study on wood degradation. *Journal of Archaeological Science* 35: 862-872.

Björdal, C.G., Nilsson, T., & Daniel, G., 1999. Microbial decay of waterlogged archaeological wood found in Sweden. *International Biodeterioration & Biodegradation* 43.1-2: 63-73.

Blanchette, R.A., Nilsson, T., Daniel, G., & Abad, A., 1990. Biological degradation of wood. In: R.M. Rowell & R.J. Barbour (eds.), *Archaeological wood: Properties, chemistry, and preservation* (Washington, D.C., American Chemical Society): 141-174.

Bonaiuti, R., 2004. Progetto di conservazione in situ del relitto romano di Procchio. *Archaeologia Maritima Mediterranea* 1: 151-156.

Camidge, K., 2009. HMS Colossus, An experimental Site Stabilization. *Conservation and Management of Archaeological Sites* 11.2: 161-188.

Cederlund, C.O., & Hocker, F., 2006. *Vasa I. The Archaeology of a Swedish Warship 1628* (Stockholm, National Maritime Museums of Sweden).

Chen, D., 2000. A monthly circulation climatology for Sweden and its application to a winter temperature case study. *International Journal of Climatology* 20: 1067-1076.

Chen, D., & Hellström, C., 1999. The influence of the North Atlantic Oscillation on the regional temperature variability in Sweden: spatial and temporal variations. *Tellus* 51A: 505-516.

Clapp, W.F., & Kenk, R., 1963. *Marine Borers; an annotated bibliography* (Washington, D.C., Office of Naval Research, Department of the Navy).

Crumlin-Pedersen, O., & Olsen, O., 2002. *The Skuldelev Ships I: Topography, History, Conservation and Display* (Roskilde, Viking Ship Museum and National Museum of Denmark).

Crump, C.B., Armbrust, E.V., & Baross, J.A., 1999. Phylogenetic analysis of particle-attached and free-living bacterial communities in the Columbia River, its estuary and the adjacent coastal ocean. *Applied and Environmental Microbiology* 65.7: 3192-3204.

Culliney, J.L., 1975. Comparative larval development of the shipworms Bankia gouldi and Teredo navalis. *Marine Biology* 29: 245-251.

Daggfeldt, B., 1963. Lybska Svan. *Tidskrift I Sjöväsendet*: 3-27.

Daniel, G.F., & Nilsson, T., 1986. Ultrastructural observations on wood degrading erosion bacteria. *The International Research Group on Wood Preservation.* Documents No: IRG/WP/1283.

Davidde, B., 2004. Methods and strategies for the conservation and museum display in situ of underwater cultural heritage. *Archaeologia Maritima Mediterranea* 1: 137-150.

Deep Sea Productions: http://www.deepsea.se/ (Accessed October 2011).

Distel, D.L., Morrill, W., MacLaren-Toussaint, N., Franks, D., & Waterbury, J., 2002. Teredinibacter turnerae gen. nov., sp nov., a dinitrogen-fixing, cellulolytic, endosymbiotic gamma-proteobacterium isolated from the gills of wood-boring molluscs (Bivalvia : Teredinidae). *International Journal of Systematic And Evolutionary Microbiology* 52: 2261-2269.

Dix, J., Rangecroft, T., Lambkin, D., Sullivan, R., Pater, C., & Oxley, I., 2009. Physical Modelling as a tool for Underwater Cultural Heritage Management. *MACHU Final Report Nr. 3*: 54-56.

Dobbs, C., 2007. Visitors, funding, and museums - reflections on the Mary Rose experience. Manage the marine cultural heritage: Defining, accessing and managing the resource. In: J. Satchell & P. Palma (eds.), *CBA research report 153* (Swindon, English Heritage): 69-77.

D'Urbano, S., Meucci, C., Nugari, M.P., & Priori, G.F., 1989. Valutazione del degrado biologico e chimico di legni archeologici in ambiente marino. In: G. Tampone (ed.), *Il Restauro del Legno,* Vol. 1 (Florence, Nardini): 79-84.

Eaton, R.A., & Hale, M.D.C., 1993. *Wood. Decay, pests and protection* (London, Chapman & Hall).

Einarsson, L., 1990. *Kronan* – underwater archaeological investigations of a 17th century man-of-war. The nature, aims and development of a maritime cultural project. *The International Journal of Nautical Archaeology* 19.4: 279-297.

Einarsson, L., 1994. *Rapport om 1994 års marinarkeologiska undersökningar av vraket efter regalskeppet Kronan* (Kalmar, Kalmar County Museum).

Einarsson, L., 1997. Artefacts from the *Kronan* (1676): categories, preservation and social structure. In: M. Redknap (ed.), *Artefacts from Wrecks* (Oxford, Oxbow): 209-218.

Einarsson, L., 2001. *Kronan* (Kalmar, Kalmar County Museum).

Einarsson, L., 2009. *Rapport om 2009 års marinarkeologiska undersökningar av vraket efter regalskeppet Kronan* (Kalmar, Kalmar County Museum).

Elken, J., & Matthäus, W., 2008. Annex A.1.1: Baltic Sea oceanography. In: BACC Author Team, *Assessment of Climate Change for the Baltic Sea Basin* (Berlin, Springer-Verlag): 379-386.

Eriksson, Ch., 2009. *Characterizing and Reconstructing 500 years of Climate in the Baltic Sea Basin*. PhD thesis, University of Gothenburg.

Ferrari, B., & Adams, J., 1990. Biogenic modifications of marine sediments and their influence on archaeological material. *International Journal of Nautical Archaeology and Underwater Exploration* 19.2: 139-151.

Fors, Y., & Björdal, C., 2009. Well-preserved shipwrecks from the Baltic Sea - a new perspective*. *Proceedings in X Nordic Theoretical Archaeology Group (Nordic TAG) Conference*. NTNU, Department of Archaeology and Religious Studies, Trondheim.

Fors, Y., Nilsson, T., & Sandström, M., 2008. Bacterial sulfur accumulation in pine (Pinus sylvestris) in simulated seabed environment to elucidate the mechanism in marine archaeological wood. *International Biodeterioration and Biodegradation* 62: 336-347.

Frederiksen, J., & Skriver, C., 2004. *FHM 4427/4, Stinesmindevraget. Rapport vedr. besigtigelse af Stinesmindevraget* (Århus, Moesgård Museum).

Froelich, P.N., Klinkhammer, G.P., Bender, M.L., Luedtke, N.A., Heath, G.R., Cullen, D., Dauphin, P., Hammond, D., Hartman, B., & Maynard, V., 1979. Early oxidation of organic matter in pelagic sediments of the eastern equatorial Atlantic: Suboxic diagenesis. *Geochimica et Cosmochimica Acta* 43: 1075-1090.

Gianfrotta, P.A., & Pomey, P., 1981. *Archeologia subacquea: storia, tecniche, scoperte e relitti* (Milan, Arnoldo Mondadori).

Glete, J., 1977. Svenska örlogsfartyg 1521-1560. Flottans uppbyggnad under ett tekniskt brytningsskede. *Forum Navale* 31: 23-119.

Glete, J., 1994. *Navies and Nations* (Stockholm, Almqvist & Wiksell International).

Glete, J., 1999. Hur stor var Kronan? Något om stora örlogsskepp i Europa under 1600-talets senare hälft. *Forum Navale* 55: 17-25.

Glete, J., 2000. *Warfare at Sea 1500-1650. Maritime Conflicts and the Transformation of Europe* (London, Routledge).

Gregory, D.J., 1999. Re-burial of timbers in the marine environment as a means of their long-term storage: experimental studies in Lynæs Sands, Denmark. *International Journal of Nautical Archaeology* 27.4: 343-358.

Gregory, D.J., 2004. Data loggers. *MoSS Newsletter* 2: 8-9.

Gregory, D., 2007. Environmental monitoring. Reburial and analyses of archaeological remains. Studies on the effects of reburial on archaeological materials performed in Marstrand, Sweden 2002-2005. In: T. Bergstrand & I.N. Godfrey (eds.), *The RAAR project* (Uddevalla, Bohusläns Museum) 20: 59-90.

Gregory, D., Jensen, P., Matthiesen, H., & Strætkvern, K., 2007. The correlation between bulk density and shock resistance of waterlogged archaeological wood using the Pilodyn. *Studies in Conservation* 52: 289-298.

Gregory, D., Ringgaard, R., & Dencker, J., 2008. From a grain of sand a mountain appears. Sediment transport and entrapment to facilitate the in situ stabilisation of exposed wreck sites. *Maritime Newsletter from Denmark* 23: 15-23.

Grenier, R., Nutley, D., & Cochran, I. (eds.), 2006. *Heritage at Risk, Special Issue: Underwater Cultural Heritage at Risk. Managing Natural and Human Impacts* (Paris, ICOMOS).

Gustafsson, B.G., & Andersson, H.C., 2001. Modeling the exchange of the Baltic Sea from the meridional atmospheric pressure difference across the North Sea. *Journal of Geophysical Research* 106(C9): 19731-19744.

Hagberg, B., Dahm, J., & Douglas, C., 2008. *Shipwrecks of the Baltic* (Stockholm, Deep Sea Productions & Prisma).

Hänninen, J., Vuorinen, I., & Hjelt, P., 2000. Climatic factors in the Atlantic control the oceanographic and ecological changes in the Baltic Sea. *Limnology & Oceanography* 45.3: 703-710.

Haygreen, J.G., & Bowyer, J.L., 1989. *Forest products and wood science* (Ames, IA, Iowa State University Press).

Hedges, J.I., 1990. The chemistry of archaeological wood. In: R.M. Rowell & R.J. Barbour (eds.), *Archaeological Wood* (Washington, D.C., American Chemical Society): 111-140.

van der Heijden, C., 2004. *Rampen en plagen in Nederland 1400 – 1940* (Zaltbommel, Kempen Uitgevers).

HELCOM (Helsinki Commission), 2009. *Eutrophication in the Baltic Sea.* Baltic Sea Environment Proceedings No. 115B. (Helsinki, Helsinki Commission).

HELCOM data base: www.helcom.fi (Accessed October 2011).

Helms, A.C., 2008. *Bacterial Diversity in Waterlogged Archaeological Wood.* Unpublished PhD thesis, The Danish Technical University, Bio Centrum, Lyngby, Denmark.

Helms, A.C., Martiny, A.C., Hofan-Bang, J., Ahring, B.K., Kilstrup, M., 2004. Identification of bacterial cultures from archaeological wood using molecular biological techniques. *International Biodeterioration & Biodegradation* 53(2): 79-88.

Henningsson, M., 1976. Degradation of wood by some fungi from the Baltic and the West coast of Sweden. *Material und organismen. Beihefte* 3: 509-519.

Hoagland, K.E., 1986. Effects of temperature, salinity, and substratum on larvae of the shipworms Teredo bartschi Clapp and T. navalis Linnaeus (Bivalvia: Teredinidae). *American Malacological Bulletin* 4.1: 89-99.

Hocker, F., 2000. Relocating the Kolding cog. *Maritime Archaeology Newsletter from Roskilde, Denmark* 14: 50-55.

Hoffman, P., 2009. On the efficiency of stabilisation methods for large waterlogged wooden objects and how to choose a method. In: K. Strætkvern & D.J. Huisman (eds.), *Proceedings of the 10th ICOM Group on Wet Organic Archaeological Materials Conference*. Nederlandse Archaeologische Rapporten 37 (Amersfoort, Rijksdienst voor Archeologie, Cultuurlandschap en Monumenten): 323-350.

Hoffmann, P., 2011, Correction, Stabilisation and Presentation: the fourth phase of the Bremen Cog project. *International Journal of Nautical Archaeology* 40: 151-161.

Howard, E.T., & Manwiller, F.G., 1969. Anatomical characteristics of southern pine stemwood. *Wood Science* 2(2): 77-86.

Huisman, D.J., Manders, M.R., Kretschmar, E., Klaassen, R.K.W.M., & Lamersdorf, N., 2008. Burial conditions and wood degradation on archaeological sites in the Netherlands. *International Biodeterioration and Biodegradation* 61: 33-44.

Hunter, K., 2004. The Newport Ship: The first two years. In: P. Hoffmann, et al. (eds.), *Proceedings of the 9th ICOM Group on Wet Organic Archaeological Materials Conference, Copenhagen 2004*, ICOM-WOAM: 411-428.

Hyde, K.D., & Pointing, S.B., 2000. *Marine mycology. A practical approach* (Hong Kong, Fungal Diversity Press).

Jacobeit, J., Jönsson, P., Bärring, L., Beck, C., & Ekström, M., 2001. Zonal indices for Europe 1780–1995 and running correlation with temperature. *Climatic Change* 48: 219-241.

Jensen, P., & Gregory, D.J., 2006. Selected physical parameters to characterize the state of preservation of waterlogged archaeological wood: A practical guide for their determination. *Journal of Archaeological Science* 33: 551-559.

Jensen, J.B., Kuijpers, A., Bennike, O., & Lemke, W., 2002. Balkat, The Baltic Sea without frontiers. *Geologi, nyt fra GEUS* 4: 1-19.

Jézégou, M.-P., 2007. Découvertes sous-marines le long du littoral des Pyrénées-Orientales. In: J. Kotarba, G. Castellvi, & Fl. Mazière (eds.), *Carte Archeologique de la Gaule, Les Pyrénées-Orientales,* 66 (Paris, Académie des Inscriptions et Belles-Lettres): 622-642.

Jöns, H., 2004. Safeguarding the Darsser Cog. *MoSS Newsletter* 3: 8-11.

Jöns, H., et al., 2003. Theme: the Darsser Cog. *MoSS Newsletter* 2:II. (http://www.nba.fi/internat/moss/download/moss_newsletter3.pdf; Accessed October 2011).

Kallio, H., 2006. The evolution of the Baltic Sea – changing shorelines and unique coasts. *Geological Survey of Finland, Special Paper* 41: 17-21.

Kim, Y.S., & Singh, A.P., 2000. Micromorphological characteristics of wood biodegradation in wet environments: a review. *IAWA J* 21.2: 135-155.

Kohlmeyer, J., 1980. Bacterial attack on wood and cellophane in the deep sea. In: T.A. Oxley, G. Becker & D. Allsopp (eds.), *Biodeterioration, Proceedings of the 4th International Symposium, Berlin* (London, Pitman & Biodeterioration Society): 187-192.

Kohlmeyer, J., & Kohlmeyer, E., 1979. *Marine Mycology, the higher fungi* (London, Academic Press Inc).

Korver, A.P.E., 2009. *De grote paalwormplaag van de 18de eeuw en de verandering van de Nederlandse dijken* (www.pieterkorver.nl/paalwormpdf.pdf; Accessed June 2011).

Kristensen, E., 1969. Attacks by Teredo Navalis L. in inner Danish waters in relation to environmental factors. *Videnskabelige meddelelser fra Dansk Naturhistorisk Forening* 132: 199-210.

Landy, E.T., & Michell, J.I., Hotchkiss, S., & Eaton, R.A., 2008. Bacterial diversity associated with archaeological waterlogged wood: Ribosomal RNA clone libraries and denaturing gradient gel electrophoresis (DGGE). *International Biodeterioration & Biodegradation* 61: 106-116.

Leino, M., Ruuskanen, A., Flinkman, J., Kaasinen, J., Klemelä, U., Hietala, R., & Nappu, N., 2011. The natural environment of the shipwreck *Vrouw Maria* (1771) in the Northern Baltic Sea: an assessment of her state of preservation. *International Journal of Nautical Archaeology* 40.1: 133-150.

Leppäranta, M., & Myrberg, K., 2008. *Physical Oceanography of the Baltic Sea*. (Berlin, Springer Praxis Books).

Lindström, M. (ed.), 1998. *The Marine Archaeology of the Baltic Sea Area. Conditions in the present, possibilities and problems in the future. Proceedings of the first meeting of the International Marine Archaeological Conference of the Baltic Sea* (Stockholm, Södertörns Högskola Research Reports 1).

Loosanoff, V.L., & Davis, H.C., 1963. *Rearing of bivalve mollusks* (London, Academic Press).

Macchioni, N., 2003. Physical characteristics of the wood from the excavations of the ancient port of Pisa. *Journal of Cultural Heritage* 4: 85-89.

MACHU Project Wreck ID: http://www.machuproject.eu/machu_cms/index.php?mode=standalone_viewer&wreck_id=64&puid=0(Accessed October 2011).

Manders, M., 2004. The Safeguarding of BZN 10. *MoSS Newsletter* 3: 6-8.

Manders, M.R., 2006. The in situ protection of a 17th century trading vessel in the Netherlands. In: R. Grenier, D. Nutley & I. Cochran (eds.), *Heritage at Risk, Special Issue: Underwater Cultural Heritage at Risk. Managing Natural and Human Impacts* (Paris, ICOMOS): 70-72.

Manders, M.R., 2006a. The in situ protection of a Dutch colonial vessel in Sri Lankan Waters. In: R. Grenier, D. Nutley & I. Cochran (eds.), *Heritage at Risk, Special Issue: Underwater Cultural Heritage at Risk. Managing Natural and Human Impacts* (Paris, ICOMOS): 58-60.

Manders, M.R., 2006b. The in situ protection of a 17th century trading vessel in the Netherlands. In: R. Grenier, D. Nutley & I. Cochran (eds.), *Heritage at Risk, Special Issue: Underwater Cultural Heritage at Risk. Managing Natural and Human Impacts* (Paris, ICOMOS): 70-72.

Manders, M., 2010. Multibeam recording as a way to monitor shipwreck sites. In: M. Manders, et al. (eds.), *MACHU Final report Nr. 3* (RCE Amersfoort): 59-66.

Manders, M., Gregory, D., & Richards, V., 2008. The in-situ preservation of archaeological sites underwater: an evaluation of some techniques. In: E. May, M. Jones & J. Mitchel (eds.), *Heritage Microbiology and Science. Microbes, Monuments and Maritime Materials* (London, The Royal Society of Chemistry): 179-204.

Mann, R., & Gallager, S.M., 1985. Growth, morphometry and biochemical composition of the wood boring molluscs Teredo navalis L., Bankia gouldi (Bartsch), and Nototeredo knoxi (Bartsch) (Bivalvia: Teredinidae). *Journal of Experimental Marine Biology and Ecology* 85.3: 229-251.

Mann, R., & Gallager, S.M., 1985. Physiological and biochemical energetics of larvae of Teredo navalis L. and Bankia gouldi (Bartsch) (Bivalvia: Teredinidae). *Journal of Experimental Marine Biology and Ecology* 85.3: 211-228.

Marsden, P., 1985. *The wreck of the Amsterdam* (London, Hutchinson).

Marsden, P., 2003. *Sealed by Time: The Loss and Recovery of the Mary Rose.* The Archaeology of the Mary Rose, Vol. 1 (Portsmouth, England, The Mary Rose Trust Ltd.).

Massuet, M.D., 1733. *Wetenswaardig onderzoek over den oorsprongk, de voortteling de ontzwachteling, het maaksel, de gedaante, de gesteltheit, den arbeidt, en de verbazende menigte der verscheidene soorten van kokerwurmen, die de Dykpalen en Schepen van enige der Vereenigde Nederlandsche Provintsien doorboren* (Amsterdam, Adriaan Wor).

Matthaus, W., & Franck, H., 1992. Characteristics of major Baltic inflows – a statistical analysis. *Continental Shelf Research* 12: 1375-1400.

Meese, D., 1771. *Verhandeling over de paalwormen zynde een antwoord op de vrage ... Hoedanig is de natuur, aart en voortteeling der wormen? ... Welk is het best, gemaklykst en minst kostbaar middel om het hout-werk op den duur daar voor te beveiligen? / Door ...David Meese, hortulanus ... aan wie de præmie van 30 goude ducaten op den 1 july 1770. is toegewezen* (Amsterdam, Flor. Liber Artes).

Meier, H.E.M., & Gustafsson, B.G., 2009. Vad styr saltvatteninbrotten till Östersjön? *Havet 2009*: 19-23.

M´Gonigle, R.H., 1926. A further consideration of the relation between distribution of Teredo navalis (Linne), and the temperature and salinity of its environment. *Natural Resources Council, Canada Report* 20: 31.

Møhlenberg, F., 2002. Pæleorm - en stor gene i havnene. *Vand og Jord* 9: 96-98.

Mouzouras, R., 1989. Soft rot decay of wood by marine microfungi. *Journal of the Institute of Wood Science* 11.5: 193-201.

Mouzouras, R., et al., 1986. Decay of wood by micro-organisms in marine environments. *B.W.P.A. Annual convention 1986.*

Nair, N.B., & Saraswarthy, M., 1971. The biology of wood-boring teredinid molluscs. *Advances in Marine Biology* 9: 335-509.

Neguerela, I., 2000. Managing the maritime heritage: the National Maritime Archaeological Museum and National Centre for Underwater Research, Cartagena, Spain. *International Journal of Nautical Archaeology* 29.2: 179-198.

Norman, E., 1977. The geographical distribution and the growth of the wood-boring molluscs Teredo navalis L., Psiloteredo megotara (Hanley) and Xylophaga dorsalis (Turton) on the Swedish west coast. *Ophelia* 16.2: 233-250.

Nystrom Godfrey, I., Bergstrand, T., Bohm, C., Christensson, E., Gregory, D., Peacock, E.E., Richards, V., & MacLeod, I., in press. Reburial and Analyses of Archaeological Remains – The RAAR project Phase II. Project status and new findings. *ICOM WOAM conference* (Greenville, SC).

Olsson, A., 2009. Some reflections on underwater cultural heritage management. In: M. Manders, et al. (eds.), *MACHU Final report Nr. 2* (RCE Amersfoort): 48-50.

Omstedt, A., & Chen, D., 2001. Influence of atmospheric circulation on the maximum ice extent in the Baltic Sea. *Journal of Geophysical Research* 106(C3): 4493-4500.

Omstedt, A., Elken, J., Lehmann, A., & Piechura, J., 2004a. Knowledge of the Baltic Sea Physics gained during the BALTEX and related programmes. *Progress In Oceanography* 63: 1-28.

Omstedt, A., Pettersen, C., Rodhe, J., & Winsor, P., 2004b. Baltic Sea climate: 200 yr of data on air temperature, sea level variation, ice cover, and atmospheric circulation. *Climate Research* 25: 205-216.

Oxley, I., 1998. The in situ preservation of underwater sites. In M. Corfield, P. Hinton, T. Nixon & M. Pollard (eds.), *Preserving archaeological remains in situ. Proceedings of the conference of 1st-3rd April, 1996* (London, Museum of London Archaeology Service; Bradford: University of Bradford, Dept. of Archaeological Sciences): 159-173.

Palma, P., 2004. Final report for the monitoring theme of the MoSS project. In: C.O. Cederlund (ed.), *MoSS Final Report* (Helsinki, National Board of Antiquities): 8-37.

Palma, P., 2009. Environmental study for the in situ protection and preservation of shipwrecks: the case of the Swash Channel wreck. *Ars Nautica, 7-9 September 2009, Dubrovnik* (unpublished; available on-line: http://eprints.bournemouth.ac.uk/11141/; Accessed June 2011).

Panshin, A.J., & Zeeuw, C.D., 1980. *Textbook of Wood Technology* (New York, McGraw-Hill).

Parker, A.J., 1992. *Ancient shipwrecks of the Mediterranean & the Roman Provinces* (Oxford, Archaeopress).

Plets, R.M.K., Dix, J.K., Adams, J.R., Bull, J.M., Henstock, T.J., Gutowski, M., & Best, A.I., 2009. The use of high-resolution 3D Chirp sub-bottom profiler for the reconstruction of the shallow water archaeological site of the Grace Dieu (1439), River Hamble. *Journal of Archaeological Science* 36: 408-418.

Pointing, S.B., & Hyde, K.D., 2000. Lignocellulose degrading marine fungi. *Biofouling* 15.1-3: 221-229.

Pomey, P., 1998. Remarques sur la conservation 'in situ' du bois de quelques épaves antiques de Méditérranée. In: C. Bonnot-Diconne, X. Hiron, Q. Khôi Tran & P. Hoffman (eds.), *Proceedings of the 7th ICOM-CC Working Group, Wet Organic Archaeological Materials Conference, Grenoble 1998* (Grenoble, Arc-Nucléart): 53-57.

Pournou, A., 2010. *The Preservation State of Waterlogged Wood from a Roman Shipwreck at Pag island, Croatia* (Athens, unpublished report).

Pournou, A., Jones, A.M., & Moss, S.T., 2001. Biodeterioration dynamics of marine wreck-sites determine the need for their in situ protection. *International Journal of Nautical Archaeology* 30.2: 299-305.

Pournou, A., Jones, A.M., & Moss, T., 1998. In situ Protection of the Zakynthos Wreck. In: C. Bonnot-Diconne, X. Hiron, Q. Khôi Tran & P. Hoffman (eds.), *Proceedings of the 7th ICOM-CC Working Group, Wet Organic Archaeological Materials Conference, Grenoble 1998* (Grenoble, Arc-Nucléart): 58-64.

Quinn, R. 2006. The role of scour in shipwreck site formation processes and the preservation of wreck-associated scour signatures in the sedimentary record. *Journal of Archaeological Science* 33(10): 1419-1432.

Quinn, R., Adams, J.R., Dix, J.K., & Bull, J.M., 1998. The *Invincible* (1758) site - an integrated geophysical assessment. *International Journal of Nautical Archaeology* 27.3: 126-138.

Quinn, R., Bull, J.M., Dix, J.K., & Adams, J.R., 1997. The *Mary Rose* site - geophysical evidence for palaeo-scour marks. *International Journal of Nautical Archaeology* 26.1: 3-16.

Rasmussen, H., & Jörgensen, B.B., 1992. Microelectrode studies of seasonal oxygen uptake in a coastal sediment: role of molecular diffusion. *Marine ecology progress series* 81: 289-303.

Richards, V., Godfrey, I., Blanchette, R., Held, B., Gregory, D., & Reed, E., 2009. In situ monitoring and stabilisation of the James Matthews shipwreck. In: K. Strætkvern & D.J. Huisman (eds.), *Proceedings of the 10th ICOM Group on Wet Organic Archaeological Materials Conference*. Nederlandse Archaeologische Rapporten 37 (Amersfoort, Rijksdienst voor Archeologie, Cultuurlandschap en Monumenten): 113-160.

Rieck, F., 1993. A Baltic Coastal Vessel – Latest Research on the wreck of a 17th century Merchant Ship at Stinesminde, Mariager Fjord, Denmark. *VIII International Baltic Seminar, 5.-7. July 1990* (Kotka, Provincial Museum of Kymenlaakso): 137-144.

Roch, F., 1932. Einige Beobachtungen zur Ökologie und physiologie von Teredo navalis L. *Arkiv for zoology* 24.A5: 1-17.

Rönnby, J., & Adams, J., 1994. *Östersjöns Sjunkna Skepp* (Stockholm, Tiden).

Rousset de Miss, J., 1733. *Aanmerkingen over den oorsprong, gesteltheit, en aard der zee-wormen die de schepen en paal-werken doorboren* (Leiden, Gysbert Langerak).

Rowell, R.M., 2005. *Handbook of wood chemistry and wood composites* (New York, Taylor & Francis).

Rule, N., 1989. Direct Survey Method and its Application Underwater. *International Journal of Nautical Archaeology* 18.2: 157-162.

Rullkötter, J., 2000. Organic Matter: The Driving Force for Early Diagenesis. In: H.D. Schulz & M. Zabel (eds.), *Marine Geochemistry* (Berlin, Springer-Verlag): 129-153.

Salisbury, W., 1966. Early Tonnage Measurement in England. *Mariner's Mirror* 52.1: 41-51.

Sandström, M., 2003. *The Kronan. XANAS of oak surface. Report on isolated analysis of oak plank from Kronan* (Stockholm, Stockholm University).

Savory, J.G., 1954. Breakdown of timber by ascomycetes and fungi imperfecti. *Annals of Applied Biology* 41(2): 336-347.

Schinke, H., & Matthäus, W., 1999. On the causes of major Baltic inflows – an analysis of long time series. *Continental Shelf Research* 18.1: 67-97.

Schulz, H.D., 2000. Redox Measurements in Marine Sediments. In: J. Schűring, H.D. Schulz, W.R. Fischer, J. Böttcher & W.H.N. Duijnisveld (eds.), *Redox: Fundamentals, Processes and Applications* (Berlin, Springer Verlag): 235-246.

Sellius, G., 1733. *Natuurkundige histori van den zeehoutworm, ofte houtvreeter, zijnde koker- en meerschelpigh: inzonderheit van den Nederlantschen* (Utrecht, Besseling).

Sleeswyk, A.W., 2003. *De Goudeneeuw van het Fluitschip* (Franeker, Uitgeverij Van Wijnen).

Sordyl, V.H., Boensch, R., Gercken, J., Gosselck, F., Kreuzberg, M., & Schulze, H., 1998. Dispersal and reproduction of the shipworm Teredo navalis L. in coastal waters of Mecklenburg-Western Pomerania. *Deutsche Gewaesserkundliche Mitteilungen* 42.4: 142-149.

Soulsby, R., 1997. *Dynamics of Marine Sands, A manual for practical applications* (London, Thomas Telford).

Steenstrup Kristensen, E., 1979. Observations on growth and life cycle of the ship-worm Teredo navalis L. (Bivalvia, Mollusca) in the Isefjord, Denmark. *Ophelia* 18.2: 235-242.

Stewart, J., Murdock, L.D., & Wadell, P., 1995. Reburial of the Red Bay wreck as a form of preservation and protection of the historic resource. In: P.B. Vandiver, J.R. Druzik, J.L.G. Madrid, I.C. Freestone & G.S. Wheeler (eds.), *Materials Issues in Art and Archaeology IV. May 16-21, 1994, Cancun, Mexico* (Pittsburgh, Materials Research Society): 791-805.

Steyne, H., 2009. Cegrass, sand & marine habitats: a sustainable future for the William Salthouse. In: V. Richards & J. McKinnon (eds.), *Public, Professionals and Preservation: Conservation of Cultural Heritage. Archaeology from Below: Engaging the Public. AIMA/ASHA/AAMH Conference 24-28th September 2008, Adelaide* (Adelaide, Australian Historical Society): 40-49.

Tikkanen, M., & Oksanen, J., 2002. Late Weichselian and Holocene shore displacement history of the Baltic Sea in Finland. *Fennia, International Journal of Geography* 180: 1-2.

Turner, R.D., 1966. *A Survey and Illustrated Catalogue of the Teredinidae* (Cambridge, MA, Museum of Comparative Zoology, Harvard University).

Turner, R.D., & Johnson, A.C., 1971. Biology of Marine Wood Boring Mollusks of the World. In: E. B. Gareth Jones & S. K. Eltringham (eds.), *Marine borers, fungi and fouling organisms of wood. Proceedings of the OECD Workshop Organised by the Committee Investigating the Preservation of Wood in the Marine Environment, 27th March-3rd April, 1968* (Paris, Organisation for Economic Co-operation and Development): 18-64.

Uścinowicz, S., 2006. A relative sea-level curve for the Polish Southern Baltic Sea. *Quaternary International* 145-146: 86-105.

Vrolik, W., Harting, P., Storm Buysing, D.J., van Oordt, J.W.L., & van Baumhauer, E.H., 1860. *Verslag over den paalworm* (Amsterdam, Natuurkundige afdeeling der Koninklijke Nederlandsche Akademie van Wetenschappen).

Wessman, S., 2003. The documentation and reconstruction of the wreck of *Vrouw Maria. MoSS Newsletter* 2003.1: 14-17.

Wessman, S., 2004. The reconstruction of *Vrouw Maria*: Building a ship from upwards down. In: C.O. Cederlund (ed.), *MoSS Final Report* (Helsinki, National Board of Antiquities): 61-63.

Winsor, P., Rodhe, J., & Omstedt, A., 2001. Baltic Sea ocean climate: An analysis of 100 yr of hydrographic data with focus on freshwater budget. *Climate Research* 18: 5-15.

Witsen, N., 1671. *Aeloude en Hedendaegsche Scheeps-Bouw en Bestier* (Amsterdam, Casparus Commelijn).

Witsen, N., 1690 (2ⁿᵈedn). *Architecturanavalisetreginemnauticum (Aeloude en hedendaegschescheepsbouw en bestier, 1671)* (Amsterdam, Pieter en Joan Blaeu).

Wood-handbook, 2010. *Wood handbook - Wood as an engineering material*. Gen.Tech. Rep. FPL-GTR-190 (Madison WI, Department of Agriculture, Forst Service, Forest Products Laboratory).

van Yk, C., 1697. *De Nederlandsche Scheeps-Bouw-Konst Open gestelt* (Delft, Andries Voorstad).

Zettersten, A., 1903. *Svenska Flottans Historia. Åren 1635-1680* (Stockholm, J. Seligmann).

List of authors

Assoc. Prof. Charlotte Gjelstrup Björdal
Coordinator of **WreckProtect**
Department of Conservation
University of Gothenburg
Box 130
405 30 Gothenburg
Sweden
Charlotte.bjordal@conservation.gu.se
www.conservation.gu.se

Mr. Martijn Manders
Cultural Heritage Agency
Smallepad 5
PO Box 1600
3800 Amersfoort
the Netherlands
M.Manders@cultureelerfgoed.nl
www.cultureelerfgoed.nl

Ms. Christin Appelqvist
Dept. of Marine Ecology - Tjärnö
University of Gothenburg, Tjärnö
452 96 Strömstad
Sweden
Christin.Appelqvist@marecol.gu.se
www.marecol.gu.se

Mr. Jörgen Dencker
Viking Ship Museum
Vindeboder 12
4000 Roskilde
Denmark
jd@vikingeskibsmuseet.dk
www.vikingeskibsmuseet.dk

Mr. Lars Einarsson
Kalmar läns Museum
P.O. Box 104
391 21 Kalmar
Sweden
lars.einarsson@kalmarlansmuseum.se
www.kalmarlansmuseum.se

Dr. David Gregory
National Museum of Denmark
I.C. Modewegsvej
2800 Kongens Lyngby
Denmark
david.john.gregory@natmus.dk
www.nationalmuseet.dk

Dr. Zyad Al Hamdani
The Geological Survey of
Denmark and Greenland
Øster Voldgade 10
1350 Copenhagen
Denmark
azk@geus.dk
www.geus.dk

Mr. Stefan Wessman
Museiverket
Marinarkeologiska enheten
Vrakholmen
00570 Helsingfors
Finland
Stefan.Wessman@nba.fi
www.nba.fi

Prof. Johan Rönnby
Maritime Archaeological Research
Institute (MARIS)
Södertörn University
141 89 Huddinge
Sweden
johan.ronnby@sh.se
www.sh.se/maris

Prof. Jon Adams
Archaeology
University of Southampton
Avenue Campus, Highfield
SO17 1BF Southampton
England
jjra@soton.ac.uk

Dr. Giulia Boetto
Archéologie navale et maritime
Centre Camille Jullian
(Aix-Marseille Université-CNRS)
Maison Méditerranéenne des
Sciences de l'Homme
5, rue du Château de l'Horloge
BP647-13094 Aix-en-Provence
Cedex 2, France
boetto@mmsh.univ-aix.fr
http://ccj.univ-provence.fr

Mr. Vincent de Bruyn
Saxion University
Polstraat 26
74 KB Deventer
The Netherlands
Vincentdebruyn.vdb@gmail.com

Acknowledgements

We would like to thank colleagues from the consortium member insitutions have also contributed to data collection, literature review and com-menting on earlier drafts of this work and other publications generated throughout the life of the project. We would particularly like to thank: Prof. Jon Havenhand, Dr. Yvonne Fors, Prof. emeritus Thomas Nilsson, Poul Jensen, Kristiane Strætkvern, Nanna Bjergaard Petersen, Morten Johansen, Mikkel Haugstrup Thomsen, Dr. Athena Trakadas, Bertil van Os, Johan Opdebeeck, Gerjo van der Meulen, and Roel Kramer. We are grateful to Astrid Brandt Grau and Michel Chapuis, European commission, directorate I, Environment, for their genuine support througout the project.